COMMUNICATING

SKILLS FOR SUCCESS

LEADERSHIP:
The Key to Management Success
by L. Bittel

MANAGING YOURSELF:
How to Control Emotion, Stress, and Time
by A. Goodloe, J. Bensahel, and J. Kelly

COMMUNICATING:
How to Organize Meetings and Presentations
by J. Callanan

HIRING THE RIGHT PERSON FOR THE RIGHT JOB
by C. Dobrish, R. Wolff, and B. Zevnik

MORALE AND MOTIVATION:
How to Measure Morale and Increase Productivity
by E. Benge and J. Hickey

JOSEPH A. CALLANAN

COMMUNICATING

HOW TO ORGANIZE MEETINGS AND PRESENTATIONS

FRANKLIN WATTS

New York   London   Toronto   Sydney

Library of Congress Cataloging in Publication Data

Callanan, Joseph A.
  Communicating—how to organize
meetings and presentations.

  Includes index.
  1. Communication in management.   2. Meetings.
3. Public speaking.   I. Title.
HF5718.C24   1984   658.4'563   84-7562
ISBN 0-531-09575-4

CONTENTS

**PART II
POWER SPEECHES AND
PRESENTATIONS**

EXHIBITS

PREFACE

Many managers view the prospect of yet another interminable business meeting with the same enthusiasm they reserve for fighting Monday-morning commuter traffic or returning to work after a vacation.

And they'd much rather perform the twelve labors of Hercules than make a critical speech or deliver a crucial presentation before an exacting audience.

Yet these two complementary management functions—meetings and speaking—are the linchpins to the extraordinary success enjoyed by many of today's highest level executives.

The interlocking of the skills involved is obvious. Without a solid grasp of the key tools used by superior speakers, your meetings may indeed be dull, boring, and unproductive. And without a smoothly run meeting as a forum, you'd have no opportunity to display your superior speaking talents.

By becoming accomplished in both areas, you'll produce immediate, positive results. Command new levels of respect and win increased support among peers and colleagues. Enjoy renewed enthusiasm and loyalty among subordinates. And best of all, stamp yourself in the eyes of top management as a rising corporate star—executive material—a future leader of the firm.

It's not an easy task. But the personal profits are enormous. You'll earmark yourself for expanded responsibilities...more frequent promotions...larger salary increases...increased corporate clout...all the necessary ingredients to propel your career on the fast track to future success.

That's what this book is all about. Making you a virtuoso performer in two of the most important personal skills an up-and-coming manager can possess: the skills of conducting and participating in meetings and speaking before groups.

MEETINGS FROM A TO Z

Part I of this book covers everything you need to know to increase the productivity and effectiveness of every meeting you will ever be involved in—from one-to-one discussions to interdepartmental sessions to company-wide conferences.

Whether you're a meeting leader or participant; at a formal presentation or impromptu bull session; in front of a group of peers or the company's board of directors—this book will show you how to turn each of those meetings from an exercise in tedium to a lively and thought-provoking idea exchange.

And the text does that in a straightforward and down-to-earth manner. No catchy euphemisms or trendy gimmicks. No academic theories or "think tank" proposals. No ivory tower strategies.

Instead, proven tips. Immediately usable suggestions. Eminently practical advice. All delivered in forms, lists, and logical steps that have weathered the test of actual business application.

Here's just a brief glimpse of some of the action material culled from business experts across the country.

Checklists on:

- meeting preparation

- post-meeting evaluation

- meeting leader analysis

- pre- and post-conference activities

Tips on:

- running a report meeting

- giving and getting feedback

- phrases that stifle discussion and those that don't

- improving your listening skills

- handling nonparticipants, conflict generators, and non-stop talkers

Suggestions for:

- 10 occasions that call for a meeting and 6 that don't

- 17 steps to a better meeting

- 8 guidelines for brainstorming

- 12 methods for handling the meeting dissident

THERE'S MORE TO COME

This list could go on and on. But that's just the beginning. For in Part II, you'll dicover all the practical advice you'll need to analyze, prepare, and deliver the most compelling speeches of your life at those meetings. Whether you're facing one client, two subordinates, three colleagues—or a conference hall full of strangers.

You'll replace insecurity and indecisiveness with confidence and persuasiveness. You'll have audiences eating out of the palm of your hand, hanging on your every word. You'll turn each speaking opportunity into a showcase for your individual talents.

Among the resources you'll find in Part II to help you realize those goals are:

- a system for rating your own speeches

- checklists for audience analysis

- tips on handling print media and TV interviews

- suggestions for utilizing props

- the do's and don'ts of off-the-cuff remarks

- steps to credibility in speechmaking

- tips on overcoming stage fright

- and much more

Communications: How to Organize Meetings and Presentations will serve as your guide through the corporate jungle as you make your way to that corner office with the big bay windows and oak door. Turn to Chapter 1 and begin that journey now.

PART I

GETTING ORGANIZED

THE
WELL-PLANNED
MEETING

"A lot of needless discussion!"

"I'm too busy to waste my time with this nonsense!"

"Now what was *that* all about?"

It's easy to recognize the subject of these complaints—business meetings. Few would argue the fact that business meetings constitute an essential tool of management. But, even so, they tend to have a shaky reputation. Too many meetings don't work very well. Instead of clarifying issues and creating ideas that lead to sound decisions, many business meetings spread confusion, nurture indecision, and produce little but irritation on the part of the participants.

Not all business meetings have these attributes. Just some. The purpose of this book is to help you turn those *some* into *none*. It's a worthwhile project because good meetings bring forth the best in people—the best ideas (often refined and sharpened by group interaction), the best decisions (often hammered out and molded by the collective wisdom of the ablest minds), and the best follow-up reactions (keyed to the prime objectives fashioned from those ideas and decisions).

THE ADVANTAGES OF A MEETING

"The meeting is the center pin of business and industry," says Frank Snell, a retired director of the international advertising agency Batton, Barton, Durstine and Osborne. According to Snell, a meeting is:

- the fastest way to pass information to a group of people;

- the best way to be positive that everyone understands equally well what has been presented and the best way to hold misunderstandings to a minimum;

- a method to receive immediate reactions, get results from a pooling of ideas that can be aired and discussed at one time by all concerned;

- a sound way to reduce tensions and resolve conflicts by bringing them out in the open; and,

- most important, by drawing on the thinking of many people, the soundest way to solve problems, produce decisions, and materially reduce the chances of being wrong.

Recognizing these advantages, many corporations are making extensive efforts to instruct their employees in the techniques of effective meetings. The Xerox Corporation, for example, distributed a film titled *Meetings, Bloody Meetings*, a lively dramatization that presented a five-step formula for correcting the characteristic weaknesses of business meetings:

1. Plan the objectives of each meeting

2. Distribute a written agenda two days before the meeting to inform participants of the objectives

3. Arrange the items to be discussed in a logical sequence

4. Control the meeting so that participants stay on the subject

5. Summarize and record the results at the meeting's end

These are the fundamentals. As a special consultant on human resources with Digital Equipment Corporation, Susan Lotz took an even more detailed look at what constitutes a good meeting. She prepared the following recommendations.

Setting Clear Objectives

To make the objectives of a meeting perfectly clear in everyone's mind before a meeting starts, answer these questions:

1. What is the subject area or agenda?

2. What are the objectives for each part of the agenda?

3. What preparation is required?

4. Who is attending and what are their roles?

5. What is the expected outcome of the meeting?

Creating a Positive Climate

The climate or tone of a meeting is set by both the physical setting and the behavior of the participants. A pleasant setting with comfortable chairs and good lighting and ventilation tends to put people at ease. People feel more a part of a group if they are in a circle and can see each other than if they are in straight rows facing the front of the room. Even with a large group of fifty or more, chairs can be arranged to facilitate group interaction.

The climate of a meeting is also affected by behavior. If people are comfortable with each other and with what's expected of them, they will participate more freely and be more productive in meetings. It is well worth taking some time at the beginning of meetings to let the group warm up and to be sure that everyone knows something about one another. People will not be completely productive if they are worrying about what is expected of them.

Assuming Proper Roles

The leader of a meeting should always begin by reviewing the agenda and the objectives and asking if anything needs to be clarified. His/her problem is then to move the group forward to meet the objectives and to facilitate constructive participation.

Leadership functions include:

- summarizing the position of the group on an issue

- getting the group to focus on the task

- deciding who talks at what point

- seeking to narrow differences and achieve consensus

- announcing decisions

Leadership can be shared in a group so that these roles are performed by all members. The more this is done, the more the members feel a sense of commitment both to the meeting process and its outcome.

Determining Decision-making Responsibility

It should be clear in any group how decisions will be made: by majority vote, by consensus, or by the leader. As decisions are made, they should be stated or written down to be sure that everyone understands and agrees. It is helpful to do this on a blackboard or easel so that everyone sees, agrees, and feels responsible to support the decision. If this is not done, decisions can be undone later by dissatisfied group members.

Reviewing Meeting Results

At the end of each meeting, a group should spend a few minutes critiquing or reviewing its work together. It should ask questions such as:

1. What did we do well?

2. What didn't we do well?

3. Did we really do what we set out to do?

4. What can be learned from today's meeting to improve the next one?

If this seems like overkill, just think about all the time you spend in meetings. It's more than you probably realize—a staff of 12 that meets 2 hours a week for 50 weeks a year involves 1,200 person-hours of time. Devoting a few minutes at the end of each meeting to improving its effectiveness should eventually lead to more productive meetings and a more effective use of your time.

IS THIS MEETING NECESSARY?

Bert Y. Auger, who worked on meeting techniques for thirty-three years with the Minnesota Mining and Manufacturing Company (3M), offers advice on three key questions to be answered before calling a meeting: when to call one, when not to call one, and who should participate.

When to Call a Meeting

1. To receive reports from participants

2. To reach a group judgment as the basis for a decision

3. To discover, analyze, or solve a problem

4. To gain acceptability for an idea, a program, or a decision

5. To achieve a training objective

6. To reconcile conflicting views

7. To provide essential information for work guidance or for the relief of insecurities or tensions

8. To assure equal understanding of company policy, methods, or decisions

9. To obtain immediate reactions when speedy response to a problem is important

10. To focus on a subject that has been neglected for a period of time

When Not to Call a Meeting

1. When other communications, such as telephone, tele-gram, letter, or memo, will produce the desired results

2. When there is not sufficient time for adequate prepa-ration by participants or leader

3. When one or more key participants is not available

4. When timing is not right

5. When the meeting is not likely to produce satisfactory results in view of clashing personalities or overall man-agement strategy

6. When expected results do not warrant spending the money it will cost to hold the meeting

Who Should Participate

1. Individuals or their departments who are expected to carry out a decision to be reached

2. One who can contribute unique information

3. One whose approval for the decision may be needed

4. One who has an official responsibility for the matter under discussion

5. One who has a personal contribution to make from a strategic standpoint

FORMAL MEETINGS

Many good business meetings cannot be placed into clearly defined categories, as you'll see in Chapters 2 and 4. But most formal meetings generally fall into one of four basic types: the problem-solving meeting, the decision-making meeting, the creative (or development) meeting, and the report meeting.

There's a big difference between a meeting called to make a decision and one that's merely intended to share information. When participants arrive at a meeting with different sets of expectations, you'll hear, "I thought this was going to be a reporting session. I didn't know we'd have to make a decision," or, "I didn't know I was going to have to make a presentation. I'm not prepared." It's much easier to be clear about the purpose of the meeting in advance than to clear up differing expectations after the meeting starts.

THE PROBLEM-SOLVING MEETING

A "problem" is any situation you want to change—confusion over a new set of company regulations, a job vacancy that needs to be filled, an unexplained drop in sales in a particular region. The key ingredient in all problems is the desire to make a change. In problem-solving meetings, it's important that all participants understand that need for change.

Tip: Usually it's best to put the problem in the form of a question. For example, "What can we do to improve sales in the northeast region?"

THE DECISION-MAKING MEETING

A decision-making meeting is one in which there is a clear mandate for the participants to take some action. This action component differentiates decision making from problem solving because the element of decision carries with it a degree of risk for all members of the group. In small meetings—such as staff or an executive committee—decisions usually are arrived at by consensus. Occasionally meeting leaders make the decision after hearing all the arguments. A formal vote is taken in business meetings only when the number of participants clearly requires it.

Tip: When you are the leader and have made up your mind before a meeting about a course of action, don't pretend it's a decision-making meeting. Your people will almost always know when they are being used merely to agree to the inevitable. That attitude will alienate your group and discourage active participation in future meetings. Simply call an information-sharing meeting and announce your decision. As you move higher in the corporate hierarchy, you'll find yourself in this position more often.

THE CREATIVE MEETING

The creative meeting deals mainly in ideas and concepts. It is particularly suited, but not restricted, to advertising groups, new product development groups, and merchandising departments. Many engineering and production groups also need creative meetings so that new ideas can be discussed, modified, and refined by interaction of the participants.

The key to a creative meeting is guidance but not rigid control. The subject should be clearly stated and the discussion kept brief and to the point. Simple language should be encouraged, and clarifications should be made by examples, illustrations, and comparisons. Stress the positive and listen to all suggestions. Chapter 4 offers a potpourri of ideas on running a creative meeting, from brainstorming to nominal-grouping techniques.

THE REPORT MEETING

Many regular staff meetings are information-sharing or reporting sessions. According to most meetings specialists, these types of meetings are often misused. Much of the reporting could be done on a one-to-one basis or in writing. You can read a report far faster and with greater retention than when you hear it at a meeting. Often the purpose of report meetings is simply to check up on whether the staff is doing its job. Listening to someone give a routine report is almost always a waste of time.

Sometimes a report is used to spot problems to be dealt with by an entire group. Subsequent problem-solving sessions may result.

Many specialists believe that report meetings should be run in an authoritarian manner because the purpose is to pass along information as concisely and as efficiently as possible. Consequently, the leader should exercise tight control. The report meeting provides data such as "the latest information on the production timetable," "current shipments' delivery dates," "expectations for distribution in the southwest district."

Brooks Fenno, a Boston, Massachusetts, marketing and sales consultant, offers these tips on report meetings.

1. Be sure speakers have sufficient time to prepare their reports—two or three days at a minimum.

2. Be specific about the theme of the meeting. Everyone must be working in the same direction, aiming for the same goal, and considering details on the same subject.

3. Be sure each member knows exactly the area he is responsible for.

4. Urge that the reports be spoken, not read. Notes, of course, can be used.

5. State the goal and stress efficiency with a clear, short opening statement.

6. Do not fall into unnecessary discussion; discourage lengthy elaboration; request brief statements of fact, opinion, decision.

7. Report on your feet. It makes for a better presentation.

8. Use visual aids. A chart, pictograph, or diagram can promote directness and clarity.

9. At the end of the meeting, state the next action to be taken.

THE COMBINATION MEETING

Many meetings contain some reporting, some creativity, some problem solving, and some decision making. Such meetings may work well as long as the roles and procedures change to accommodate the varying modes.

"Meetings get into trouble when transitions are sloppy," said Michael Doyle, a former executive of Interaction Associates of San Francisco, specialists in organizational development. "If in the middle of a report someone asks a question, which produces a problem that leads to an argument, the result can be a meeting in shambles. People may leave the meeting stunned, wondering how things went from a report to a shouting match."

If you think that a report meeting may switch to a problem-solving meeting, be on the alert for the transition. Try to make sure that everyone present agrees to tackle the problem at that particular time. Later, if there is a jump from problem solving to decision making, determine whether it is possible to make a decision and, if so, who is going to make it and how. Don't just let "one thing lead to another" to the extent that control is lost.

No matter what type of meeting you're involved in—from formal to creative to combination—the checklist in Exhibit 1 will lay a good foundation for a productive session.

IDEAL ATTENDANCE FIGURES

Opinions vary about the optimum attendance at business meetings. But it's generally agreed that *the dynamics of a meeting change and become more complex as the size expands*. Meetings of more than 15 people require formal procedures and rules. Hands have to be raised for any kind of interaction, and the meeting becomes less spontaneous. The conclusion of many experts is that report meetings work well with larger groups, but that meetings designed to make decisions, solve problems, or generate creativity should be confined to no more than 15 participants.

Frank Snell offers the following guides to the size of business meetings:

1. Try to limit the number of participants to 15. Any larger meeting is difficult to control. The leader finds it unwieldy and difficult to pursue the steps necessary for the successful group examination and solution of problems. Since the purpose of the meeting is to draw on

EXHIBIT 1.

Checklist for Meeting Preparation

Have you:

- ☐ Fixed in your mind the objectives to be attained through the meeting discussion?
- ☐ Secured, prepared, or thoroughly familiarized yourself with the necessary meeting aids?
  - ☐ Charts ready?
  - ☐ Case studies prepared?
  - ☐ Fact sheets to be distributed ready in sufficient quantities?
  - ☐ Demonstrations predetermined?
  - ☐ All special materials obtained?
  - ☐ Films to be used previewed and a plan made for their use?
- ☐ Prepared your opening presentation?
- ☐ Carefully studied your meeting outline?
  - ☐ Determined the important points to be emphasized?
  - ☐ Considered anticipated responses and group reactions?
  - ☐ Determined points at which quick summaries will be made?
  - ☐ Considered experiences and stories to be used for emphasis?
  - ☐ Determined ways and means of initiating conferee participation, stimulating thinking, and creating interest?
  - ☐ Considered what the summary of the group's thinking might be?

☐ Planned carefully to be sure adequate time has been allotted?

☐ Notified everyone concerned of time and place of meeting?

☐ Checked physical requirements of meeting place?

　☐ Blackboard or chart paper available?

　☐ Seating arrangement conforms to good meeting procedure?

　☐ Facilities for showing films in readiness?

　☐ Ashtrays provided if smoking is permissible?

　☐ Chalk, crayon, thumbtacks, erasers, paper, pencils, etc., on hand?

　☐ Ventilation, heat, light, conferee comfort adequate?

---

the thinking of all present, it is obvious that the large meeting slows progress.

2.   Limit the representatives from each department. Discourage the tendency of a department manager to bring several assistants. This doubling up in meetings is costly, unwieldy, and unnecessary. It is one more barrier to direct, efficient decisions. One department representative is enough—don't have two!

3.   Urge each department representative to bring the point of view of his or her department. This is one of the reasons a complete agenda is so important. When the people to be present at your meeting have a clear picture of the problem to be discussed, they can easily hold a pre-meeting discussion within their own departments.

This will result in contributions that are definite, direct, and constructive. Do the same for your department.

4. Be sure each representative has the authority to make the decision for his or her department. No meeting can succeed if the members do not have that authority. The meeting is basically action-oriented, designed to mold facts and ideas into the resolution of a problem.

"There will be times when it is impossible to live by the suggestion that meetings be confined to fifteen participants," Snell acknowledges. "If you must have a large group, make an adjustment to fit the situation. Break down the group into smaller units (six is a good size). Make each group examine the problem and come to a decision. Then have each group send a representative to a final group meeting. This technique breaks an unwieldy mass down into compact working groups."

PLANNING AND WRITING AN AGENDA

A prime ingredient for an effective meeting is an agenda. Everyone should know what to expect before coming to a meeting. If all the participants receive an agenda at least a day (preferably two or three) before the meeting, they will come prepared, and most of the common causes of confusion and misdirection will be avoided.

Exhibit 2 shows a simple agenda for a meeting designed to come to a decision about the packaging of a new product. By showing the subject, persons attending, reason and goal, and so on, an agenda allows participants to form opinions, gather information, and prepare to participate. Result: shorter, more effective meetings.

EXHIBIT 2.

A Simple Agenda

Agenda

Date: October 31, 19—
From: Mike Corrigan

Date of meeting: November 3, 19—

Place: Room 206

Subject: New packaging for Omnitex

Estimated time: One hour

Attended by: Chaffee, Fishbein, Salinger, Benvenuto

Background: Omnitex can now be packaged more creatively because of modifications in product design and production techniques.

Reason for meeting: Marketing research shows that present package design is ineffective on display shelves.

Goal of meeting: To decide on new package design for Omnitex.

Some companies supply forms to help meeting leaders to plan and write an agenda. Exhibit 3 provides an agenda form that covers all the important considerations. You may find it helpful to make copies of this form for your own use and that of others in your company when they conduct meetings. You'll stand out as an even more professional meeting organizer.

EXHIBIT 3.

An All-Purpose Agenda

Agenda

Name of group _____ Date _____

Title of meeting _____ Starting time _____

Called by _____ Place _____

Purpose of meeting _____

Background materials _____

Please bring _____

Desired outcomes _____

Manager/Chairperson _____ Recorder _____

Group members _____

Order of agenda items	Time allocated
1. _____	_____
2. _____	_____
3. _____	_____
4. _____	_____
5. _____	_____

The main fault of many agendas is that they are vague. For example, the phrase "development budget" relays little information. A longer explanation—"To discuss the proposal for reduction of the 1984–1985 development budget now that the introduction of our new product has been postponed"—helps all meeting members to form some views or even develop facts and figures in advance.

Meeting leaders should not be afraid of a long agenda, provided the length results from a thorough analysis and definition of each item rather than from the addition of more items than the meeting can reasonably consider in the time allowed. Leaders should include, very briefly, some indication of the reason for each topic to be discussed. An item of special interest should be singled out for special mention in a covering note.

PREPARING MEETING MINUTES

It's useful to have one member of a meeting take the minutes, because this task requires a strong sense of what's important. Although a secretary often does the job, responsibility for the minutes remains with the leader. He or she should see that the following facts are included:

- The time and date of the meeting, where it was held, and who chaired it

- Names of all present and indications of absences

- All agenda items (and others) discussed and all decisions reached; if action was agreed on, record (and underline) the name of the person responsible for the assignment

- The time at which the meeting ended (important, because it may be significant later to know whether the discussion lasted 15 minutes or 6 hours)

- The date, time, and place of the next meeting

Exhibit 4 provides a general form for writing the minutes of your meetings. When you have a series of meetings attacking a specific problem, record the results in one place

EXHIBIT 4.

Form for minutes of a meeting

Minutes

NAME: _____ TITLE: _____ DATE: _____

What happened and how:

Decisions/Action items:

Next steps:

This group memo is my interpretation of what happened at this meeting. If you would like to correct an error, make an addition, consult the original tape recording, or receive a transcribed copy of the tape, please call _____. For more information concerning the objectives of the meeting and who attended it, see the attached agenda.

Recorder _____

with cumulative minutes that show the various steps taken over a period of time.

Exhibit 5, an after-meeting checklist, provides a measuring device with which to judge the meeting just held. And it serves as a reminder of what can be upgraded to improve your next meeting.

Exhibit 6 will hit a little closer to home. It is an after-meeting evaluation of the meeting leader and how he or she conducted the interaction. If you're intent on honing your skills, distribute copies of Exhibit 6 after your next meeting and ask for some honest assessments.

EXHIBIT 5.

A post-meeting evaluation checklist

	Yes	No
1. Was the agenda well prepared and sent to members in advance?	_____	_____
2. Was the purpose of the meeting clear to all? Were the objectives clearly specified?	_____	_____
3. Was the type of meeting appropriate to the task?	_____	_____
4. If it was a problem-solving meeting, did everyone recognize and accept the problem being addressed?	_____	_____
5. If it was a decision-making meeting, did everyone accept how the decision was made?	_____	_____

6. Were the right people involved—people with the relevant expertise who had primary responsibility and authority to make the decision?   ____ ____

7. Was the size of the group appropriate for the type of meeting being held?   ____ ____

8. Were feedback and disagreement encouraged?   ____ ____

9. Did the meeting stay on topic?   ____ ____

10. Did the leader exercise the proper amount of control?   ____ ____

11. Did the participants become actively involved?   ____ ____

12. Did the meeting accomplish anything?   ____ ____

13. How well did the leader handle difficult situations?   ____ ____

14. Were plans made to address unfinished business?

EXHIBIT 6.

A post-meeting leadership evaluation form

EVALUATION FORM

Program title _____ Date _____

Leader _____

Please answer the questions below. You need not identify yourself. How would you rate the following?

	Excellent	Satisfactory	Unsatisfactory
Ability of leader	____	____	____
Adequacy of program content	____	____	____
Adequacy of visual and audio aids	____	____	____
Adequacy of materials	____	____	____
Application to your job	____	____	____
Conduct of session	____	____	____
Length of program	____	____	____
Adequacy of facilities	____	____	____

If any factor is rated "unsatisfactory," please explain:

_____

_____

What did you find most valuable?

_____

_____

What was least valuable to you?

_____

_____

Additional comments:

_____

_____

_____

_____
Signature (optional)

OPENING THE LINES FOR FEEDBACK

One of the most critical tests of your communications effectiveness is how well your audience understands—and responds to—your message. How do you judge? Feedback. Preparing a feedback mechanism for your meeting should be one of your initial moves. Here are eight guidelines to ensure useful and productive feedback. Give the guidelines to everyone attending so they will "feed back" properly also.

1. Make feedback descriptive rather than evaluative or judgmental. Describe your own reaction. Let the group and individuals accept or reject it in the spirit in which it was given—professionally. By avoiding evaluative language, you reduce the likelihood of a defensive response.

2. Make feedback specific rather than general. To tell a participant that he or she is "dominating" accomplishes little. The overactive participant might be better advised to listen more attentively to others and allow them to have their say.

3. Recognize that feedback involves the needs of both giver and receiver. It can be destructive when it is offered as a one-way street, a "my way or the highway" reaction.

4. Direct behavior toward a specific action or function or process. Make sure the receiver of the feedback can do something about it. You only increase frustration when your feedback involves something over which the receiver has no control.

5. Try to have the feedback solicited rather than imposed. It is most useful when the receiver has asked for it.

6. See that the feedback is well timed. In general, it's most useful at the earliest opportunity. Reacting in a June meeting to a problem that occurred in February doesn't do much for the immediacy of the feedback—or your meeting. Timing also depends on the person's readiness to hear it.

7. Check to ensure clear communication. The best way is to have the receiver of the feedback "feed-back" to the dispenser. See if they are on the same wavelength.

8. Use other parties to check on the accuracy of feedback. Is it one person's impression of what was stated, or does everyone get the same picture? Use this device at the meeting to get everything clear before it breaks up.

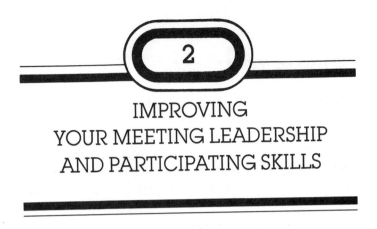

IMPROVING
YOUR MEETING LEADERSHIP
AND PARTICIPATING SKILLS

As a meeting leader, you must devote sufficient time and energy to give it your best. If you're too busy, too overly distracted by other pressing business problems to give a meeting your best effort, you should postpone calling it.

The effective leader enjoys discussions and is a good speaker. You'll become one by following the suggestions in Part II of this book. Leaders' skills include planning the agenda, creating a climate that assures participation by the members, and controlling the discussion so that all who want to be heard can be heard.

You should also make sure that the group stays reasonably close to the agenda.

Tip: Put the highpoints of the agenda on a flip chart that is visible to all participants. The leader should also be able to make spur-of-the-moment adjustments to permit useful detours. The main concern, though, is to keep the discussion on course.

DUTIES OF THE LEADER

As a leader you should make both the purpose and the goal of the meeting clear to the group. Is it a decision-making meeting, problem solving, report, or creative?

Introduce members who do not know one another. Draw out silent participants. Keep an eye out for members who tend to monopolize the discussion and keep track of time. Keep the discussion on track. Often it's also your job to relieve tensions, especially in groups that don't meet often. You must handle all comments and questions in a way that encourages members to make more contributions.

THE TECHNIQUES OF LEADERSHIP

The three basic techniques for managing a meeting are: the question, the summary, and the directive.

Questions often help start a discussion. Phrase them in such a way that they cannot be answered with a "yes" or a "no." "What do you think of the new promotion plan, Jack?" is a good example. Usually an open-ended question asks for information, an opinion, or a suggestion. Such questions are most effective at the early stages of a meeting. The leader should quickly establish that the comments should be short and to the point. If the first speaker runs on too long, the leader can then ask a direct question of another member.

Summaries can also be used to keep the meeting headed in the right direction. In a brief summary, you can emphasize the topic on the agenda and tactfully suggest that the group is veering away from the topic. You can also use the summary as a way to move to another item on the agenda if you feel the meeting is faltering because enough has already been said on the subject.

The direct approach is sometimes the best. Simply point out to the participants that they are moving away from the subject. For example, "We seem to be getting away from the main point here. Let's get back to what Mary was talking about." Or, "This is interesting, but it really doesn't help much in regard to the question of who is responsible." Or, "I've been listening to this discussion and wondering how it ties in. We have to get back to the basic question that Joe asked earlier."

Move the meeting along. Watch for signs that an item has been discussed enough. Quite often, a loss of interest or a drifting from the subject is a clue. The summary is probably the most useful technique in keeping a meeting moving. You can finish an agenda item and lead naturally to the next topic with a summary. You can also use questions to learn whether enough time has been devoted to the subject. "Perhaps it's time to move on to the next item on the agenda. What do you think?"

In decision-making meetings, the leader can be of great help if he/she makes an observation about the consensus. "I think we're in agreement. Is anybody against the reorganization of the filing system?"

As a leader, you can also help the majority reach a decision by suggesting a vote. In most business meetings such a vote can be handled informally by an expression of agreement or disagreement or a simple nodding of heads or raising of hands. In larger meetings, leaders should clearly state the issue and then ask for affirmative or negative votes. They may take a voice vote or ask for a show of hands. Some organizations have provisions for secret ballots or for roll-call votes on important matters. In any case, a leader should always announce the voting results.

Handling Digressions

The biggest problem for the leader of a business meeting is the tendency of groups to wander from the subject at hand. Sometimes such discussions lead to important matters that appear elsewhere on the agenda or matters that were overlooked in preparing the agenda.

In such cases, it's wise to be flexible and let the important topics be resolved. The skillful leader senses when he/she should let the meeting wander a little. But frequent digressions waste time. Meetings must be brought back to the topic.

Again, questions help do this. You may ask, "Can we tie this in with the point about the quality-control standards?" Or, "Just a moment, Bob, how does this relate to the problem of slow deliveries?" Or, "Let's see now. You're getting confused. Where are we in relation to overtime pay to assembly workers?"

Handling Garrulous Participants

Another common problem is the member who talks too much. This is a delicate situation demanding tact. If you are too brusque in stopping the talkative member, you may embarrass the other participants and sound antagonistic.

An effective technique is to ask yes-no questions of the vociferous member and then quickly direct an open-ended question to another participant. Here's an example:

Leader: Just a minute, Pete, would you be willing to drop that account completely?

Pete: Now, I didn't say . . .

Leader: I just want to be clear on this. Would you favor that?

Pete: Well, no, but . . .

Leader: [interrupting] Jane, I wonder how you feel about this?

A person dominating a meeting may speak on an abstract level. He or she can usually be stopped by a question that asks for specific information or for an example. An illustration:

Tony: There are altogether too many people around here who are not pulling their weight. Too many of those guys in production are just putting in their time . . .

Leader: [interrupting] Excuse me, Tony, but could you give us an example of what you mean?

Summaries can also be used to stop lengthy discussions. If the leader breaks in with a summary, the dominant member will often sit back and give him or her the floor. Then the leader can conclude the summary by directing a question to another member, thereby tactfully cutting off the talkative member.

As a leader, you will be forced occasionally to simply direct the member to stop talking. You might say, "That's an important point. Let's get the reaction of some of the rest of us on that." Or, "Just a minute. You have raised three or four points. Before you go any further I would like to spend a little more time on this question of responsibility. What do the rest of you think about that?" Or, "I'm going to ask you to stop there for a minute and hold your next comment. The entire group has not yet had a chance to be heard on this point. Let's hear from everyone and then we'll come back to you."

Handling Noncontributing Members

The member who rarely says anything is almost as difficult as the talkative one. You will probably have to use questions to deal with him or her. Address the person by name and ask a direct question. Don't ask a question that will elicit a one-word answer. Try to ask a question that you're sure the silent person can answer. The best course: ask for an opinion, not for specific information or examples. Here are some good questions for evoking responsive answers:

"Jim, what do you think about this proposal?"

"Jim, where do you stand on the quality-control problem?"

"Jim, we haven't heard from you about this yet. What do you think?"

Handling Conflicts

The leader is responsible for dealing with all conflicts that arise in a meeting. *It is very important that you do not take sides.* If asked your opinion on a conflict, avoid dealing directly with the issue by relaying the question to the group. "That's a tough one. Will anyone take a crack at it?" Or bounce the question back to the questioner. "Let me ask you how you would answer the same question?" The main point is not to be dragged into the conflict. As a participant in the fight, you lose control of the meeting.

When several members come into conflict, the leader should interrupt and focus the attention of the meeting on the group procedure rather than on the individuals involved. Remind the group of areas of agreement. Admit that intelligent and conscientious people often differ and that it's desirable for everyone to express his or her opinion. Emphasize the importance of the ideas, rather than the personalities. Remind the group that differences about ideas often lead to the best kind of creativity. Humor helps in such situations, too.

Chapter 5 provides more insights into the ticklish situations you must address when handling conflict in meetings.

Handling the Meeting Dissident

No matter what position of power you eventually attain, you'll always run into the "meeting dissident." Here are some tips for handling that negative and aggravating individual.

1. Listen—ask open questions to get at truthful answers about feelings and ideas. You may be surprised to find yourself agreeing to some of the dissident's contentions.

2. Take the dissident aside and find out why he or she is really there. Maybe his or her negative reaction isn't really aimed at you. Perhaps you can divert it in the right direction.

3. Give the problem only the attention it deserves. You can't allow the rest of the meeting participants to suffer.

4. Negotiate—even though this only neutralizes, rather than solves, the problem, at least you can get on with the meeting.

5. Positively reinforce constructive ideas and behaviors. Make the dissident feel better about acceptance behaviors. Direct him or her away from the disruptive.

6. Break into small groups if the meeting must go on and you can't neutralize him or her.

7. Ignore the problem. Again, not a solution, but it may buy you some time. If the negativism vanishes, your problem is solved.

8. Smother the dissident with attention—briefly. See if you can channel the dissident's divergence into a constructive mode by making him or her "minority leader."

9. Cut the dissident down to size. Use your wit and superior knowledge of the subject and meeting dynamics to put the dissident in his or her place.

10. Use your power as leader and tell the dissident to stifle it. This establishes your position as leader, but doesn't do much for your reputation as a tactful handler of people.

11. Throw the bum out. If it comes down to him/her or you, you know who has to go—and quickly.

TIPS ON MEETING LEADERSHIP

Bob Leiban, while a training consultant for Red Lion Motor Inns, a chain of motels across the United States, made a study of leadership skills in business meetings. "Skillful questioning," he says, "is the leader's most useful tool. Of course, no one can tell you what questions to ask or how to ask them. That depends on your topics, your personnel, and yourself."

Leiban does offer the following guidelines for improving your leadership skills:

1. Sometimes it is well to ask an elementary question just to get the discussion started. It will get the group talking, and then the conversation should flow naturally.

2. Avoid answering your own questions. The meeting leader generally has more knowledge of the subject than the group. This makes it tempting to follow a question with a lengthy answer—an excellent way to prevent discussion.

3. Ask only questions that are within the ability of the group to answer. Avoid the philosophical or technically complicated question.

4. Avoid questions that will annoy the group, or that are arrogant or sarcastic.

5. Always ask for the experience of group members—everyone is an expert in his or her own field.

6. In extreme situations, follow your questions with a long silence. This will become so embarrassing that someone will speak up, just to relieve the tension. This method is especially useful with a group that is slow in starting. But only employ it as a last resort.

7. Before deciding what steps to take about talkative members, try to figure out why they act this way. Are they trying to impress the group or the boss? Do they have a personal grudge? Is it just their nature? Maybe they think faster than the others and have more ideas and experience.

8. Using your leadership skills to draw out the quiet member is usually acceptable. But some people have deeply rooted reasons for their reticence. It is better to let such persons alone. Let them listen.

9. Be aware that your handling of ideas from the group can either stimulate or stifle discussion. When one person makes a comment or offers an idea, it sets the others thinking. This usually starts a chain of ideas and discussion. Your job as leader is to guide this discussion toward the goal of the meeting.

10. Listen attentively to everything that's said. Listen with your mind as well as your ears. Nothing is more discouraging to group members than to feel that the leader isn't listening to them. You'll find a wealth of listening tips in Chapter 3.

11. Be patient. Some of the best participants are slow in expressing themselves in a group. They must be coached, encouraged, cajoled. Others will talk around the issue. Still others will misunderstand the question or opinion. The astute leader is aware of these common failings.

12. Protect the members from laughter or derision. One way to do this is to switch the attention to another idea. Or rephrase a comment or question so that you are identified with it. By doing this, you can keep it from being considered a "foolish remark." Above all, never cut a person short, even though you think he or she is wrong.

RATING YOURSELF AS A MEETING LEADER

Self-assessment often helps in improving skills. Use Exhibit 7 to evaluate yourself as a group leader. Score yourself "good," "average," or "poor" in the categories listed.

Taking this method one step further, it may be helpful to ask a trusted subordinate or colleague who is a regular participant at your meetings to fill out a similar question-

EXHIBIT 7.

Leader self-evaluation checklist

	GOOD	AVERAGE	POOR
1. Initiating goals and procedures to help groups organize their meetings.	____	____	____
2. Seeking information, ideas, opinions from the group.	____	____	____
3. Giving information, your own views.	____	____	____
4. Summarizing different points of view.	____	____	____
5. Checking for consensus, determining areas of agreement and disagreement.	____	____	____
6. Giving assignments on action items.	____	____	____
7. Encouraging others in group.	____	____	____
8. Harmonizing relationships by reducing tensions, shedding light on personal differences.	____	____	____
9. Encouraging everyone to participate, keeping the channels of communication open.	____	____	____
10. Clarifying information by reflecting what was said.	____	____	____
11. Planning the meeting, even when agenda is unwritten.	____	____	____
12. Reviewing and acting on results of the meeting.	____	____	____

naire. If your colleague gives you an objective assessment, you can compare the two to find out where your strengths and weaknesses lie, and work on them.

Tips on Meeting Participation

You will not always be the leader of the meetings you attend. At some meetings you will be a contributing member. Your role as a member is just as vital and satisfying as your role as leader. You and your fellow members of a business meeting are as responsible as the leader for the results.

Being an effective meeting member requires a knowledge and skill of many of the same techniques employed by the effective leader. In fact, if the leader isn't as effective as he or she might be, your skills as a member can keep the meeting on track and productive.

In general, however, it's better to concentrate on the content and let the leader worry about the process of the meeting. Don't try to steer the meeting your way.

Remember: There is no single right way to solve a problem or one absolutely correct process for making a meeting work. If you're a seasoned leader, it's easy to fall into the trap of showing off your expertise and proving the leader incorrect. Focus on the problem, not the leader. Don't offer procedural advice unless you're asked for help or the leader clearly needs it.

Special Phrases That Encourage/Discourage

Just a few choice words from the meeting leader can either fire up the participants or throw a wet blanket over the proceeding.

Here are some key phrases that encourage participation.

- That's great, how can we do it?
- What else do we need to consider?
- I like that!
- How can we build on that idea?
- Keep talking, you're on the right track.
- We can do a lot with that idea.
- I think it will fly!
- Let's get right on it.
- That's an interesting challenge.
- That's an interesting idea.
- I'm glad you brought that up.
- How can we help you?

To avoid putting a damper on the meeting, shun the following phrases.

- It's not a bad idea, but...
- The problem with that idea is...
- We haven't the time!
- It's not in the budget!
- We've never done it that way before.
- Let's discuss it some other time.
- It needs more study.

- Let's form a committee.

- Has anyone else ever tried it?

- You don't understand this problem.

Physical Positioning

In groups that meet on a regular basis, don't always sit in the same place with the same people. You can develop a group that psychologically sets itself apart from the rest. By changing your position from meeting to meeting, you can help rearrange the seating patterns of others and keep the group from becoming polarized physically and psychologically.

Accentuating the Positive

Don't evaluate an idea before it has a chance to be fully explained and developed. Don't be negative. Negativism is a common human failing that says new or different or odd-sounding ideas never work.

As a group member, you'll make an outstanding contribution by helping to set a positive tone. Look for values in an idea. Don't sit poised to jump on the first sign of flaw or fault. Say what you like about an idea before you express your concerns: "What I like about your suggestion is that it could solve the employment problem, but I'm afraid of what the unions might do to us for proposing it."

Accepting Criticism

Meetings are often a battleground of egos in which the fight is to maintain personal dignity and self-esteem rather than accomplish the meeting's purpose.

As a group member, don't let yourself be dragged into petty arguments. Don't be defensive if your "great" idea is criticized. Try not to take it as a personal attack. Stay open to criticism and use it to develop your ideas further. Don't back yourself into a corner.

Don't forget, once your idea is recorded by the secretary (or whoever takes the minutes), it belongs to the group. Let it survive on its own merits. The goal is to find a solution to the problem at hand as a group. The more you identify yourself personally with the idea, the harder it is for the group to accept it on its merits.

Seventeen Steps to a Better Meeting

Following the steps outlined below will ensure the success of your next meeting, as either a leader or a participant.

Before the meeting

1. Plan the meeting carefully: who, what, when, where, why, how many.

2. Prepare and send out an agenda in advance.

3. Come early and set up the meeting room.

At the beginning of the meeting

4. Start on time.

5. Get participants to introduce themselves and state their expectations for the meeting.

6. Clearly define roles.

7. Review, revise, and order the agenda.

8. Set clear time limits.

9. Review action items from the previous meeting.

During the meeting

10. Focus on the same problem in the same way at the same time.

At the end of the meeting

11. Establish action items: who, what, when.

12. Set the date and place of the next meeting and develop a preliminary agenda.

13. Evaluate the meeting.

14. Close the meeting crisply and positively.

15. Clean up and rearrange the room.

After the meeting

16. Prepare the minutes.

17. Follow up on action items and begin to plan the next meeting.

THE MEETING LEADER
AS LISTENER

You may be reading right now, but at any minute someone is going to interrupt. Your secretary with a question on where a report goes. Your subordinate wondering what the policy is on initiating a new project. A colleague wanting to discuss a friction point between your department and his or hers.

The first thing you do is listen. Sounds so simple. But you know from experience how often people have not "heard" what you've really "said." And vice versa.

Think about your last meeting. Was any of the "information" lost in the translation because you weren't listening well? Did you emerge from it wondering just what really went on? And what's to come next?

The better a listener you are, the better your chances of hearing those magic words—"You've done such a good job, we want to give you a raise and a promotion."

PRACTICING YOUR LISTENING

Start right now. The next time a subordinate or colleague comes into your office find out just what his or her major purpose is in seeing you.

When the reason is given, make a mental note of the problem. Don't ask questions before your colleague is finished. Take a few short notes to jog your memory later. If you're unsure of the precise nature of the problem when your colleague is finished, ask for a repeat. That doesn't mean you haven't listened well. It means he or she hasn't communicated correctly.

Ask succinct questions. Never feel you have to lead the conversation, even if you're running the meeting. No matter how many people are present, don't hesitate to ask "leading" questions to make matters crystal clear. Let others explain. You ask for those explanations.

If an interruption occurs. Answer the telephone or take the message, but first tell the speaker to "hold that point." When the interruption is over, come back to the point, ask for a quick refresher, and go on. Note taking comes in handy on such occasions.

Listen for themes, not facts. Keep in mind that many people are not very good at communicating. (They probably haven't read this book!) It's up to you to extract the sum of their statements and interpolate the impact. Rather than getting bogged down in a morass of facts, cut through to the overall theme or trend in what is being presented. You'll have a better overview and perspective.

Have your secretary sit in. At important meetings or conferences, you may want to concentrate all your attention on the speaker. Taking notes will be a nuisance and may lessen your listening ability. Ask a trusted aide to take some general notes.

Don't "block out" parts of the discussion. Be very aware that your mind may wander. It may race ahead if the meeting drags along. You may be two steps ahead of the pack. But if you are, you could miss a vital ingredient.

Work on your attention span. Like any executive skill, the ability to be attentive can be improved. You know you sometimes tune people out. As soon as you become conscious of this, do something. Stretch in your seat. Suggest a short break. Walk around. Exercise will refresh your mind, remind you that you were drifting, and get you back on the right track.

WORKING AT LISTENING

To make yourself a better listener, avoid the bad habits listed below and incorporate those of the good listener.

THE BAD LISTENER	THE GOOD LISTENER
1. Tunes out dry subjects	Opportunizes and asks "What's in it for me?"
2. Judges negatively if the delivery is poor	Judges content, ignores errors in delivery
3. Becomes argumentative easily	Doesn't interject until the speaker has finished
4. Listens for particular facts	Listens for central themes
5. Takes extensive notes	Jots down mind-joggers

THE BAD LISTENER	THE GOOD LISTENER
6. Doesn't seem to be paying attention	Exhibits an active body state, maintains eye contact
7. Is easily distracted	Avoids distractions, concentrates
8. Resists difficult material and topics	Looks upon tough material as a challenge, a mental exercise
9. Reacts too emotionally	Refrains from emotional overinvolvement
10. Tends to daydream with slower speakers	Listens "between the lines" to everything that is said

TEST YOURSELF

You may have always thought of yourself as a good listener and figure that you already knew all these basic tips. Well, let's just find out with a standard quiz that has been administered to general groups of managers.

This is a three-part quiz. The first is short and sweet. Simply circle the adjective below that best describes how *you* think *you* rate as a listener. No one is looking over your shoulder, but it's important that you make the rating as objective as possible.

Superior   Excellent   Above Average
Average   Below Average   Poor   Terrible

Now on a scale of 1 to 100, give your listening ability a numerical rating. Of course, 100 is tops.

Want to know how you stack up? Almost 85% consider themselves average or less. Only 5% rate themselves superior or excellent. On the numerical scale, the general range falls between 35 and 85. The average rating is 55.

Now here's another short quiz. How would the following people in your life rate you as a listener? Again, use the 1–100 scale.

Your best friend____

Your secretary____

Your immediate subordinate____

Your spouse____

Your immediate superior____

When comparing the listening self-rating with the projected ratings of others, most people feel that their best friend would rate them highest as a good listener. And that rating is generally higher than the one they gave themselves. That seems logical, since, almost by definition, a best friend is someone eager and willing to listen to your problems.

The ratings for the subordinate and secretary are usually close. They probably think you pay attention to what they're saying, but not as much as they would like you to. The response of one's superior falls all over the lot. It generally reflects a personal relationship.

Curiously, the listening rating for one's spouse generally falls far below the personal 55 rate. Experts point to the fact that in many homes spouses talk with each other at dinner and on weekends but active listening skills just aren't emphasized.

These first two tests are subjective and fluctuation is common. Your scores may be very different from the consensus. That is not bad in itself. The third test is somewhat more complicated. It requires a self-analysis of your own bad habits. You can keep score and you'll see at the end how you rate. But the main thing is to use the list to alter those bad habits, not just to judge how often you engage in them. Check the appropriate letter, then score according to the key that follows.

1. I find the subject of a meeting uninteresting:
a. always b. usually c. sometimes d. seldom e. never

2. I criticize the speaker's delivery or mannerisms:
a. always b. usually c. sometimes d. seldom e. never

3. I get overstimulated by what the speaker says:
a. always b. usually c. sometimes d. seldom e. never

4. I listen primarily just for the facts:
a. always b. usually c. sometimes d. seldom e. never

5. I try to outline everything the speaker says:
a. always b. usually c. sometimes d. seldom e. never

6. I fake attention to the speaker:
a. always b. usually c. sometimes d. seldom e. never

7. I allow distractions to interfere:
a. always b. usually c. sometimes d. seldom e. never

8. I avoid difficult material:
a. always b. usually c. sometimes d. seldom e. never

9. I let emotionally laden words arouse personal feelings:
a. always b. usually c. sometimes d. seldom e. never

10. I waste meetings by daydreaming:
a. always b. usually c. sometimes d. seldom e. never

Key: For every "always" checked, give yourself 2 points; "usually," 4 points; "sometimes," 6; "seldom," 8; "never," 10.

Compute your total score. The average on most tests for business people is 62, 7 points higher than that earlier self-assessment average. Where do you stand?

IMPROVING YOUR LISTENING SKILLS

Here is a baker's dozen of suggestions of positive methods for improving the way you listen.

1. Give every person equal time at least—better yet, listen twice as much as you talk.

2. Listen just as intently to people you don't like who are speaking on subjects that irritate you.

3. Every person has something worthwhile to say, both your closest advisor and your biggest competitor.

4. No matter what else concerns you at the moment, concentrate on just one thing—listening to the person you're with.

5. Encourage people with verbal (questions, agreement) and nonverbal (gestures, facial expressions) feedback.

6. Be sensitive to tone, expressions, innuendos, gestures. Their meaning may be more important than words.

7. Test yourself as the meeting progresses to make sure you are "catching the drift." If not, say so.

8. Make a mental catalogue of important points, areas to probe, items to focus on later.

9. Lead into disagreements with points of agreement. Try to emphasize common interest, then debate.

10. View every dispute or conflict as an opportunity to expand your own horizons and learn something new—and maybe change for the better.

11. Switch off all negative thoughts and preconceived notions *before* the meeting begins.

12. Don't let a speaker's bad judgment or emotional reaction cause the same in you.

13. Recognize that listening is a skill—one that could catapult you higher in the corporate structure. Practice, practice, practice.

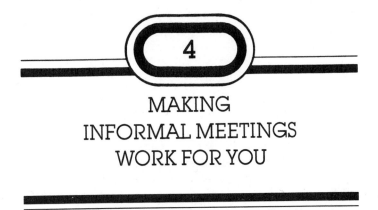

MAKING
INFORMAL MEETINGS
WORK FOR YOU

"I've had as many good meetings in the parking lot as in the conference room." You've probably heard similar comments a thousand times. Many executives also echo this sentiment. Impromptu meetings play an important role in business. They may take place anywhere—an office, hallway, restaurant, bar, golf course, parking lot. The well-planned meeting discussed in Chapter 1 comprises only part of the picture. Spontaneous, informal meetings are also an integral part of the business process. Some of the biggest deals and most important decisions have been made in the most out-of-the-way and unassuming places.

Such meetings do not have to be random and directionless. They can be used to solve problems and achieve goals in much the same way as formal meetings.

THE EVER-READY AGENDA

"I *always* have an agenda in my head," says Harry Longo, a successful Boston marketing consultant. "I never write it down, but it's there, ready for every meeting whether by chance or by appointment."

Longo's contention is that there are certain points to be made with clients and prospective clients and that you must stay alert to whatever opportunities may arise.

Many business people do this intuitively. But it always pays to think through the desirable results of even the most casual meetings. An example. Bill Thomsen, a vice president of the Multitech Corporation, lost his brilliant new advertising manager, Ted Watts, simply because he failed to prepare himself properly before telling Ted that the executive committee had rejected his institutional advertising campaign.

The conversation in Thomsen's office:

Ted: How'd it go?
Bill: Oh, they killed it. Too expensive.
Ted: Expensive! I broke my back keeping costs down!
Bill: Well, I guess, you know, they had other things on their mind.
Ted: They're not too interested in my work, eh?
Bill: Come on, Ted. That's got nothing to do with it.
Ted: I think it does. If they had liked the ads, they would have appropriated the money.
Bill: [impatiently] I'm telling you they just didn't want to spend the money at this time.

Ted then got angrier and told Bill he thought the members of the executive committee (which included Bill) were dumb. That in turn made Bill angry, and he told Ted that he'd better wake up to reality—Multitech wasn't in business to gratify his creative urges.

So Ted quit, and Bill lost the best advertising manager he ever had. The executive committee really did think the campaign was brilliant, but the company needed to concentrate its resources on product advertising for the next year or so. If Bill had prepared for his meeting with Ted, he would have made sure that Ted clearly understood the situation, and the following conversation might have taken place:

Ted: How'd it go?

Bill: They loved it. President Tullsen said it was the best advertising campaign he's ever seen for Multitech, but it's really necessary that we hold it until next year. We need to spend every penny we have on the product lines, especially the Multitech-100.

Ted: Well, I'm disappointed but I can see their point.

Bill: Got any good ideas for Multitech-100? That's where we need your help right now.

Ted: I sure do. Can we talk about them now?

Informal Meetings in Your Office

In most informal meetings in your own office, you are the leader. Often people on your staff stop in to ask questions, give casual progress reports, or relay some news.

These are meetings without an agenda, and the atmosphere is relaxed and friendly. You want to keep it that way. At the same time, you should be aware that such situations are conducive to productive thinking, especially in terms of problem solving and idea generating.

So, it's important to be a person whose "door is always open," at least to the extent that your staff knows you welcome suggestions, ideas, and proposals that they might not want to bring up at more formal meetings.

It's good strategy to have casual get-togethers in your office to attack specific problems. The more casual, the better. Just ask your secretary to invite the three or four colleagues or members of your staff who might contribute the most.

Informality sets the tone. Your people understand that they are not under pressure to be brilliant or perfect. They're there to help you solve a mutual problem. It's your job to guide the discussion to that end.

Guests in your office.   Meetings in your office attended by business visitors are always partly social in nature. You are representing your company, yet trying to make those "guests" feel comfortable.

Keep in mind that underneath the pleasantries of social exchange, such meetings also have an unwritten agenda. Both parties are there for business. Don't get stalled in personal conversation.

To avoid such a problem, look for ways to tactfully steer the conversation around to the subject. Try combining a social idea with one related to business—"I'm glad to hear your flight was smooth. Did you know that that airline uses our computer for its flight reservations?"

Meetings in other people's offices.   When a superior calls and says "Do you have a minute?" you usually don't know whether he's going to present you with a crisis in the plant or a description of how bad the traffic was coming to work that morning. There's no agenda, and you are not the leader of the meeting.

Even so, it's wise to develop a plan, no matter how uncertain. Think of the major concerns that your boss has in running the department. Review the ideas, suggestions, and plans that you may want to broach.

Remember: Every such meeting is an opportunity to

make a contribution. Your own personal agenda should always be in the back of your head, ready to be adapted to all meetings where you can make a legitimate contribution as participant as well as leader.

Lunch and Dinner Meetings

Certain meetings lend themselves to being conducted in less formal atmospheres than an office setting, such as a restaurant. A meeting called to discuss the impact of a new company policy falls into that category. So does one designed to review past decisions, establish stronger ties, or elicit opinions.

There are, however, meetings that are hampered by such circumstances. Evaluating an accounting sheet, reviewing financial results, or signing contracts are activities usually reserved for the office.

Besides informality, the advantages of meeting in a restaurant for lunch or dinner include:

- neutrality—neither party is automatically superior because of site

- fewer interruptions—the phone doesn't ring and subordinates don't rush in with problems

- timing—it's usually easier to get two busy executives together for lunch than to find an hour during the business day when they are both free

- freer conversation—the conventions of business language are usually less observed

The possible disadvantages of such meetings are:
- noise

- distractions

- poor service

- lack of space

- restrictions on paper or briefcases

- crucial information is not available

On the matter of business meetings over lunch or dinner, consultant Harry Longo has these observations:

- Be careful about the number you invite to a lunch or dinner meeting at which you intend to do serious work. You may lose control when there are more than six.

- If possible, use restaurants that you know and that know you. If that's not possible, be sure to discuss your plans with the headwaiter when you make the reservation. Your chances of good service are sure to be much improved.

- You don't have to take notes at the table. When you get back to the office, dictate a quick summary of the discussion, clearly indicating the ideas, decisions, or actions agreed upon. You can even send a copy to your guests, depending on the circumstances.

- Some business people just won't talk seriously while they're eating. When you sense this to be the case, don't be pushy. Wait until the coffee comes or arrange another meeting in the office.

- Have regular luncheons for your staff, preferably at the same table in the same restaurant. Good ideas can come out of those lunches. Sometimes when you're under a deadline, take them out to dinner. It breaks the tension.

For more advice on conducting lunch and dinner meetings, see the suggestions in Chapter 5.

The Ad Hoc Meeting

In Latin, *ad hoc* means "for this special purpose." Members of an ad hoc meeting are appointed for their particular skills or expertise or experience. They generally get together only once, to solve a special problem or to make a decision in a crisis situation, such as a plant shutdown, an unexpected disruption of parts distribution, or a similar emergency.

In such situations, both the issue and the need for co-operation are clear to all participants. Ad hoc meetings usually accomplish their purpose because the participants don't get sidetracked. Each has a stake in the resolution of the difficulty for which the meeting was called.

Some organizations, especially educational institutions, make use of an on-going ad hoc committee. Such a committee may meet on a regular basis over an extended period of time. Usually its function is to make in-depth studies of long-term matters or to keep an eye on a developing situation.

In business, an ad hoc committee may be appointed to review employee benefits, methods of capital formation, new product possibilities, or any other issue that tends to change with the times.

Getting Away: The Business Retreat

Many companies organize retreats for groups engaged in projects. The idea is to separate them from the familiar setting of an office, plant, or laboratory for two or three days to allow a discussion of ideas and problems free from the normal routines.

The purpose of these retreats is not "rest and relaxation" (though they may provide that). Rather, they are designed to attack specific projects or problems in an atmosphere free from distractions.

Usually retreats are held in quiet country inns or houses specially designed to accommodate groups of business people. According to Don Connell, who has arranged many such retreats for managers of the Marathon Oil Company, a good attendance figure is 10 to 12.

"Beyond 15, the retreat becomes a party," he says. "The group concentration is lost, and the atmosphere is more like a convention or a big conference."

Are retreats productive? "Yes," Connell says. "Unusually so. The change of setting seems to help concentration. Also, the best retreats are focused on one particular problem—new products, for instance, or budget cutting—and every member is aware that this is serious work."

Retreats without a clear purpose, Connell adds, may give your people a pleasant rest, but they don't solve problems, create ideas, or produce sound decisions.

THE ART OF BRAINSTORMING

The objectives of certain meetings demand that a premium be placed on creativity and imaginative solutions to proposed problems. The technique known as brainstorming was developed for just such circumstances. It is based on the supposition that each person has two modes of thought. The first is the freely associative and generates ideas. The second, more logical and orderly, acts as a filter.

By removing the filter, most notably the fear of ridicule by others, creativity is enhanced. Thus the two major rules of a brainstorming session are (1) any and every idea, no matter how crazy, should be expressed and (2) no criticism or evaluation is allowed until the meeting ends.

As the leader at such a meeting, here are a few guidelines that will improve your effectiveness:

1. Make sure all participants know the subject area. Cutting costs, increasing profits, and raising sales totals may be good topics, but limits should be established. For example, "How can we cut costs in our delivery department?" or "How can we maximize profits in our northeast region?"

2. Be prepared for a barrage of ideas by appointing two or three people to record them. The recorders alternate taking down the ideas.

3. Set a time limit. After about half an hour, brainstorming meetings generally slow down.

4. Give your group a goal, such as 150 ideas before the session ends.

5. Provide inspiration and encouragement. "I'm sure we all have a lot of ideas. We want to hear all of them. Here's one to start. Now let's have yours."

6. Stick to the rules. No criticism or evaluation by anyone, including yourself. "Hold on, Bill. You can react to another idea, but no judgment on it. Give us a different idea instead."

7. Keep the energy level high. Move the conversation along briskly. Draw your more reticent members out. Call them by name and make it comfortable for them to join in. Promote the informal atmosphere.

8. End the session decisively and on an enthusiastic note. "Good meeting. Let's end now. But if you hit on any more ideas, get them to me. We want to be sure to have more."

OTHER METHODS OF GENERATING NEW IDEAS

The individual or company that develops the most creative solutions to problems is the one that will succeed. When the process of brainstorming was first developed, managers quickly seized the idea and put it to work.

Yet even though brainstorming has been around since the 1960s, some who have utilized the concept are now finding a few built-in flaws. Although they recognize the advantages of brainstorming, they also point out drawbacks that cannot be avoided.

For example, the success of brainstorming depends to a large degree on the participants involved and the make-up of that group. Some managers have pointed out that brainstorming can be very time-consuming and, in some cases, expensive. Others say that brainstorming is most effective when the problems are relatively simple. And others complain that such a system works much better with "trial-and-error" techniques rather than difficult judgment decisions.

Because of these shortcomings, other processes have been developed to attack difficult problems. They have their own styles that are different from brainstorming. But they have all been tested and are successful in the appropriate forum.

Nominal Grouping Technique

Developed by Andre L. Delbecq and Andrew Van de Ven, nominal grouping technique (NGT) consists of 5 steps that can be applied to all levels of employees within an organization.

NGT tends to be much more structured than conventional brainstorming, with the emphasis more on establishing priorities and less on interpersonal interaction. Here are the 5 steps.

1. Idea listing. Each group member is instructed to list suggestions to the specific problem. These ideas are written down and should take no more than 15 minutes to compile.

2. Recording. The participants then present their ideas, which are formally recorded on a master sheet. Duplications are discarded.

3. Preliminary voting. After some discussion to clarify each idea, the participants then vote for the 5 best ideas on the list. Each participant is also asked to rank the ideas, with 5 points being given to the best idea, 4 points to the second best, and so on. The results are tabulated and those ideas with the highest scores are listed.

4. Discussion. Each idea is then deliberately discussed and dissected. Ideas can be combined or re-shaped, according to the group's feeling.

5. Final voting. After the thorough discussion in the preceding step, each member is instructed to vote again on the ideas. The votes are counted, and the highest-scoring

ideas are submitted to the appropriate committee or function.

NGT allows the participants to gain a much stronger insight into the proposed ideas and how they might work. Brainstorming tends to be superficial in scope; there is little regard for pragmatics. But with NGT, more extensive discussion suggests stronger—and more practical—solutions to problems.

DISCUSSION 66

This particular method was invented by Don Phillips, former president of Hillsdale College in Michigan. To him, the major problem with brainstorming sessions was that they led to domination by a few outspoken members while the majority of the group sat and said nothing.

To overcome this "fear" of speaking within the group, Phillips thought a new forum was needed. He decided to go with smaller groups, only six members at a time with a leader and a reporter to record the suggestions. And to stimulate discussion even more, Phillips' plan imposed a time limit on the participants.

Each group has six minutes to come up with some creative ideas to a problem. When the time limit is up, another problem is handed to the group, which has six minutes for that as well. By the time all the problems on the agenda have been covered, the pressure of the time limit combined with the smallness of the group ensure that the reporter has noted several solutions and suggestions.

In many ways, Phillips' idea makes sense, particularly because in conventional brainstorming sessions domineering personalities can alter the course of the meeting and also inhibit others. With a small group, plus the added time pressure, people lose their inhibitions and can have at least some ideas written down at the end of the time period.

THE DELPHI TECHNIQUE

This particular technique tries to take advantage of a sense of competitiveness as well as a feeling of company cooperation. Developed by the Rand Corporation, this process tends to be more time-consuming—mainly because all the interaction is done via written memos and not within one large group meeting. But you can also use this technique as the basis for a more structured meeting.

When a problem is posed, the manager who runs the Delphi technique composes a list of company "experts"— those individuals within the organization who will participate in the solution process. Each expert is given a questionnaire and asked to make written suggestions and comments on how they would solve the problem. The entire process is anonymous, so each expert has plenty of freedom to suggest almost any idea.

The questionnaires are then gathered and the opinions are compiled into a list. A second questionnaire with the same problem is circulated to the experts, but this time the compiled suggestions are included, as is a list of the experts. No names, however, are attached to the suggestions, so the process is still relatively anonymous. Each expert is now asked to read the gathered opinions and to come up with yet another suggestion—theoretically synthesized from the already compiled lists. The entire process continues until the best and most workable ideas are found. Because it is a written technique, each participant is allowed to ponder each suggestion in depth. And by assessing each idea individually, eventually a consensus on the best solution is reached.

The Gordon Technique

This method places a special emphasis upon the group leader because in this unique setting only he knows the exact problem to be solved. First developed by William J. Gordon of Arthur D. Little, Inc., a well-known business consulting firm, this approach works best with a group of six to eight "experts" who have backgrounds in different fields. The group leader steers the discussion along general guidelines without ever precisely stating the problem. Instead, he openly talks about the problems the company has had in the past in this particular area, and then he receives feedback from the group.

Eventually, the problem is revealed. But by that point, the group members have already given their thoughts on how best to approach the desired goal in general. Such a process puts a tremendous demand on the group leader because he must carefully guide the conversation in the right direction.

ADVICE ON
HANDLING SPECIFIC TYPES
OF MEETINGS

While the general suggestions and tips on conducting a productive meeting apply to the entire spectrum of group interactions, special meetings call for special preparations.

Five such specific meetings are particularly important to the progressive manager:

1. committee

2. luncheon/dinner

3. conflict resolution

4. advisory

5. training

RESEARCH ON COMMITTEE MEETINGS

At this point in your career, most of your committee work may be as a member. But as your talent grows and shows, you'll be asked to "chair" such groups. You can start your preparation for that day right now.

For many years as a psychologist at Harvard University, Robert F. Bales conducted laboratory research on how committees make decisions. He observed their operations and those of other small groups in a specially designed room equipped with a one-way glass mirror. Through it a team of psychologists could watch without disturbing the participants.

The basic research is a long, tedious, and time-consuming process that cannot be shortened by the need for practical results.

Bales nevertheless offers the following "recommendations" for setting up and directing decision-making committee meetings:

1. Limit the size of committees to seven members unless more members are absolutely necessary to obtain representation of all relevant points of view. Set up conditions of size, seating, and time allowed so that each member has an adequate opportunity to communicate *directly* with every other member.

2. Avoid appointing committees as small as two or three members if an authority problem between members is likely to be critical.

3. Choose members who are naturally moderate participators. Groups of *high* participators will suffer from competition. Groups of *low* participators may find themselves short of ideas.

4. Don't assume that a good committee is comprised of one good "leader" and several "followers." Provide the

group with both a task leader and a social leader, who will support each other. A sprinkling of knowledgeable but more silent members adds flavor to the balance of the group.

A group of balanced composition can usually absorb one "difficult" member—for example, one who talks too much, is short on problem-solving ability, tends to arouse dislikes, or cannot be changed by ordinary social pressure. The best strategy is to surround such a person with productive members—or exclude him or her completely.

5. In actual procedure, start with the facts even if you think everyone at the meeting already knows them. A short review is seldom a waste of time. A good general procedure is to deal with three questions on each major agenda item:

   • "What are the facts pertaining to the problem?"

   • "How do we feel about them?"

   • "What shall we do about them?"

   This is the preferred order. Lay the groundwork before getting to specific suggestions, the third stage. Note that the order recommended is the exact opposite of formal parliamentary procedure.

6. Solicit the opinions and experiences of others, especially when disagreements develop. People often think they disagree when actually they simply are not talking about the same experiences. In such cases, they do not interact well enough to realize that, although they are using different words, they are relating similar experiences. Try to get past the words to the experiences.

7. When another person is talking, listen and actively indicate your reactions. Other suggestions for listening are covered in Chapter 3. People can't be expected to read your mind. Besides that, they need the recognition you can give them by your honest reaction, whether positive or negative.

8. Keep your eyes on the group. When you are talking, talk to the group as a whole rather than to one of your associates or an antagonist. Much communication goes on at a nonverbal level. Nothing improves the general harmony of a group as much as a strong undercurrent of direct eye contact. Part II of this book will cover the entire spectrum of speaking strategies.

9. When you sense trouble, stop the argument and go back to the facts and direct experience. Often, the best way to get on a cooperative track again after a period of difficulty is to agree to go out and gather further facts.

10. Pay special attention to group feelings. No set of rules can substitute for constant, sensitive, and sympathetic attention to what is going on among members. Do not become so deeply involved in getting the job done that you forget the first prerequisite for success—keeping the committee in good operating condition.

CONDUCTING A CONFLICT-RESOLUTION MEETING

As more and more people are placed under your supervision, the chances of your being confronted with conflicts rise geometrically. You can prepare yourself for such an eventuality by learning how to conduct a conflict-resolution

EXHIBIT 8.

Questionnaire to use in preparing
for a conflict-resolution meeting

Questions for Participants
Prior to a Conflict-Resolution Meeting

1. What is the problem between you and the other party as
   you perceive it?

   _____

   _____

   _____

2. What does the other party do that contributes to the problem?

   _____

   _____

   _____

3. What do you do that contributes to the problem?

   _____

   _____

   _____

4. What do you want/need from the other party so as to effectively perform your job?

   _____

   _____

   _____

meeting that *really* resolves conflict. First, each party in the conflict should complete the questionnaire in Exhibit 8 as the basis for the discussion. Schedule the meeting at a neutral site where both parties feel at ease.

Allow two hours for that first meeting. You're the facilitator, the traffic cop. You must ensure that both parties get equal time to present their points of view. The last thing you want to do, especially at the start, is judge which party is right or wrong.

Your stance should be neutral, the "United Nations observer." No vested interest in having one side win the war. If your position doesn't lend itself to that, create a conflict-management team and ask one of them, or an outside consultant, to serve as third party.

Eight Tips for Success

The following eight factors are critical to the success of any conflict-resolution meeting.

1. Do spatial arrangements promote equality and avoid divisiveness? Problem solving should take place on neutral ground with parties arranged in a nonconfrontational manner. Direct attention and energy toward the problem, not the people.

   A third party moderator may want to physically realign himself or herself throughout the discussion, first with one party in the dispute, then with the other, to ensure his or her neutral role in the eyes of the participants.

2. Don't let time constraints become a consideration. Problem solving occurs most readily where the parties are not pressured by deadlines.

3. It's your job to control group size to facilitate interaction and avoid divisiveness. Groups of five to seven people are most appropriate for member satisfaction.

4. Mingling is important. Make sure the communication process is arranged so that all members communicate with each other rather than through a single group representative.

5. Your main aim as group leader is to control the *process* of group interaction rather than the *content* of discussion. Group leaders should be very familiar with the process of problem solving and should direct their attention to ensuring that all the steps in the process take place. They should not promote their own preferred solutions. You may have the "perfect" answer. Keep it to yourself.

6. Is information shared by all parties rather than hoarded by some to be used for their own advantage? Shared information promotes trust and reduces differences of power associated with monopolies of information.

7. Seize the day. Don't let opportunities to deal with problems as they occur fly by. Rather than reserving them for discussion at a later date, tackle them immediately. Delays permit facts to be lost and positions to be distorted. Problem solving is facilitated when parties can handle problems as they arise.

8. Is there a balance between concern for *production* of results and concern for *people*? In a conflict-resolution meeting, the group must allow the expression of differing ideas, feelings, and alternative solutions. Encourage your participants to work vigorously at the task of evaluating solutions and selecting the best.

Using that Pre-meeting Questionnaire

Ask one participant to state his or her answers to the four questions in Exhibit 8. No interruptions from you or the other participant. If the latter has questions, or comments, tell him or her to jot them down.

When the first participant has finished, questions can be asked, but only for understanding, not debate or innuendo.

The second participant then presents his or her answers to the four questions, and a similar "understanding" session follows.

After both parties have had a chance to get their contentions off their chests and clearly express their points of view, ask for their responses to the real action question: "What first step can *you* take to resolve this problem?"

Note: You are asking what each individual or the group can do, not what they want the other side to do.

At this point both sides should have a firm grasp of how they've each contributed to the conflict, what their interdependence entails, and what they need from the other party to effectively perform their jobs. Plus, they should recognize what they will gain from a successful resolution of the matter.

If you've done your job of moving them into this problem-solving mode—good listening and low defensive barriers—you should be well on your way to a solution.

SERVING AS AN ADVISOR

As your involvement with management increases, you will be asked to serve on advisory panels, committees, and boards—from voluntary civic committees to local public library groups to education and alumni boards to Chamber of Commerce groups and Boy Scout and Girl Scout councils.

Some business people see these as irritating diversions or unavoidable nuisances. Others feel a moral compulsion to serve on them. They are in fact opportunities to broaden your contacts, exercise your expertise, and lay the foundation for profitable future communications.

Here are a dozen leadership tips for handling these types of meetings.

1. Don't beg or coax anyone to serve. And don't accept anyone as a member unless he or she agrees to make an effort to attend all meetings. Anyone who gives a halfhearted commitment won't give you his or her best shot.

2. Avoid choosing persons who stand to profit personally from a committee's actions and those who have to clear their votes with an organization. Conflicts of interest and delays can thwart the efforts of the best-intentioned committee chairperson.

3. Don't ask an advisory committee to deal with simple problems. Give them the tough ones. The people on it should comprise your first team.

4. Limit the size of the committee to fifteen members. Too many cooks . . .

5. You don't need a whole slew of "experts" on a particular subject. You need individuals who are intelligent, objective, and in touch with the feelings of others. Like you!

6. Develop basic factual information to be hashed over at the first few committee meetings. Supply each member with detailed fact sheets.

7. Design initial meetings for clarification and understanding. Facts should dominate, not opinions.

8. After the facts, bring on the discussion. The leader, presumably you, should review any consensus and points of agreement after each "discussion" meeting.

9. The location of the meeting should not be too comfortable or attractive. The Taj Mahal will distract from the purpose: work.

10. Focus on the main goal at all times. And remember, that main goal is *not* an elaborate report. It *is* the solution to the problem being addressed.

11. Design your report with that in mind. Broaden the understanding of, but don't overwhelm, your audience.

12. Use clear, concise language in your report. You're a business person. You know how to avoid flowery and officious words. Do so.

CONDUCTING
A MAJOR CONFERENCE

You've probably attended in-house company-wide conferences. And you've probably pitied the harried executive who had to run them. Well, prepare yourself. That may be you someday!

In-house conferences are one thing. But you can just about double or triple the headaches when you take charge of an out-of-town conference. Yet many shrewd managers have used such meetings as stepping-stones to more responsibility, higher personal profiles, and better corporate positions.

More and more companies are running such meetings as incentive packages to forge closer communications among departments or to help paint a clearer overall picture of the direction in which the company should be headed.

Every company function is fertile ground for such a conference. At first you may offer to serve on the preparation committee. Then you take over one segment of the show. Finally you assume control of all aspects.

A successful conference can focus the corporate spotlight directly on your act. Whether you've ever served on a conference committee or not, you should know the nuts and bolts behind overseeing a well-run conference.

This chapter provides a step-by-step guide to planning and implementing a major event. It's designed to cover all the details and procedures you'll need to know to conduct a successful conference. It assumes that you are the leader. Because that's where you're headed!

Why Hold a Major Meeting?

Before making any decisions about time, place, theme, program, procedure, participants, or budget, stop and think about the purpose of the event. What are your objectives and goals? Can they best be achieved in this manner? Are you planning this conference to:

- pool information, exchange ideas
- build morale/confidence in the organization
- introduce a new product or service
- develop policy
- discuss long-range policies
- educate
- reach decisions, compromises, agreements
- prepare a report
- clarify issues
- negotiate

- show or seek support or approval
- develop or foster employee goodwill
- gain publicity
- improve relations with your community, customers, suppliers, government
- show public solidarity

Who Is to Attend?

At the same time, you also need to ask who will be attending the event.

Is your audience:

- employees (what levels?)
- spouses of employees
- customers
- potential customers
- suppliers
- stockholders
- competitors
- media
- general public
- people who have never attended such an event
- people who seldom attend such an event
- people who frequently attend such an event

- mostly people under 30

- mostly people under 40

- mostly people 40–60

- mostly people nearing retirement age

- all ages

- mostly men (all men?)

- mostly women (all women?)

- equal numbers of men and women

Why Is the Audience Attending?

People may be attending your event because they want to or because they're obligated to. More specific attendee objectives may be to:

- get to know top managers

- get to know fellow employees

- get to know customers and possible customers

- exchange ideas and information

- learn about a new product or service (which may increase one's commissions, etc.)

- get help in solving a problem

- show or seek approval or support

- gain publicity or attract attention

- enjoy themselves

- please their boss

It's likely that you will have more than one goal or objective for staging a conference or event. The people who come will also have more than one reason for doing so.

Thus, the organization's goals may not be the same as those of the attendees. For instance, the organization's main goal may be to introduce a new product, the attendee's to increase his/her own sales.

As a result, you will have to resist the temptation to do too much and to include too many categories of participants. (Unless, that is, you are planning a major convention or conference with hundreds, perhaps thousands, of attendees. In this case, the sheer size and diversity of the event will be one of its strengths.)

OBTAINING ASSISTANCE

Enlist help right away. A special event requires much planning, and you need time for this. Allow at least six weeks for a fairly modest conference or event—six to eight months for a big affair.

If you're planning a convention or conference that will be held in a major hotel or conference center, you'll need two to five *years'* advance notice.

Select a few key people who can help you discuss possibilities and make basic decisions. They should be people to whom you will eventually delegate responsibilities.

You may wish to limit your own role to that of making initial plans and policies. You can name someone else to supervise the actual proceedings, either another employee or an outside consultant who specializes in such events.

The chances are good, however, that you don't need outside help. Most conferences are managed by people who are handling the responsibility for the first time. Even a novice at planning a major event can obtain expert (and usually free) help from convention and conference bureaus and hotels where such events are frequently held.

LAYING THE GROUNDWORK

After you and your preliminary planning committee have decided that the conference or event should be held, and what your goals and objectives are, the next step is to organize working committees to deal with the details.

Again you should look at your company and its needs, review what events (if any) of a similar nature your organization has sponsored before, and try to isolate any special problems and concerns you'll have to resolve.

Make sure you've touched base with everyone whose approval or help you'll need. And consider these questions:

1. What part, if any, does the president want to play?

2. Should you schedule a meeting of top managers to get their ideas?

3. Do you need to meet with the treasurer to discuss your budget?

4. Who must participate in the planning?

5. What committees will you need (program, scheduling, finance, entertainment, public relations)?

DEVELOPING A PROGRAM

The purpose of the event will largely determine the program and the theme, if there is to be one. For example, a *new product* introduction should be designed to "showcase" the product and your company.

Tell:

- how it was developed
- by whom
- what it is
- what it does
- how it will be marketed
- by whom
- what effect it will have on the company

This is also a good opportunity to honor the developers of the new product.

If your purpose is to *boost employee morale* with a company-wide picnic or dinner, the program might feature informal and humorous speeches and group activities such as games, singing, and contests.

An event aimed at *customers and potential customers* generally calls for elaborate exhibits and receptions, speeches by the company president and vice president for marketing, a cocktail party, and a dinner.

An *educational program* involves lectures, workshops, and seminars, usually with an array of guest speakers and professionals. Exhibit 9 shows a tentative program developed some years ago by Exxon's Northeastern Region Marketing Department for a communicators' conference. It serves as an example of how one company approached this type of conference.

Choosing a Theme

The preliminary planning committee should also decide on a theme for the event. As convention planners Robert H.

EXHIBIT 9.

A sample conference schedule

Communicators' Conference
Sterling Forest Conference Center
Tuxedo, New York
November 28–30, 19—

Friday, November 28

4:00 p.m.	REGISTRATION
6:15 p.m.	Reception

7:00 p.m.	Dinner and Welcome
	Responsibility in Journalism
	    Michael Sheldrick,
	    Energy Editor,
	    Business Week Magazine

Saturday, November 29

8:00 a.m.	BREAKFAST

9:15 a.m.	The Mood of America Today
	    James B. Lindheim,
	    Vice President,
	    Yankelovich, Skelly & White

10:30 a.m.	BREAK

10:45 a.m.	Editing in Today's Environment
	    Panel Members:
	    Jean Richards, Editor,
	        The Millbrook Roundtable
	    Edward Mack, Editor,
	        Hunterdon County Democrat
	    Joseph M. Ungaro,
	        Vice President &
	        Executive Editor, Westchester
	        Rockland Newspapers
	    V. Don Hersam, Publisher,
	        New Canaan Advertiser

12 Noon	LUNCH
1:15 p.m.	Investigative Reporting on Public Interest Issues Gordon Bishop, Feature Writer, *The Star-Ledger*
2:15 p.m.	BREAK
2:45 p.m.	How to Use Visual Communications Effectively Philip N. Douglis, Director, The Douglis Visual Workshop
4:15 p.m.	RECESS
6:30 p.m.	RECEPTION and DINNER

Sunday, November 30

8:00 a.m.	BREAKFAST
9:15 a.m.	Energy Update Richard H. Larrabee, Planning Manager, Supply Department, Exxon Company, U.S.A.
10:15 a.m.	B R E A K
10:30 a.m.	Politics and The Press The Honorable J. J. Froude, Jr. Member, The New Jersey Assembly
11:30 a.m.	CLOSING REMARKS
12 Noon	LUNCH
	ADJOURNMENT

Drain and Neil Oakley point out, a theme is *not* an objective. A theme reinforces objectives, creating mood and atmosphere.

For example, Jubilee 350 was the theme of the conference and events sponsored by the city of Boston to celebrate its 350th birthday. "A New Environmental Ethic" was the theme of an international clean-air conference. "The Shape of the Future" was the theme of a major event held by a company to announce diversifications in its product line. The first consideration in theme selection, according to Drain and Oakley, is the occasion. A theme must always be appropriate to the occasion. "Smiting Smog in the '80s," for instance, was considered as a theme for the clean-air conference. But it was discarded as being too frivolous for a gathering of distinguished scientists from many countries and cultures.

Once a theme has been decided upon, it is used on any of the preconference materials that are mailed out, especially in the form of logo and slogan. It should also be promptly displayed at the event on badges, signs, displays, and so on.

Selecting Speakers and Speeches

The purpose of the event will determine your program, and the program will determine your speakers.

You may invite a company official or top manager to discuss some major change, policy, or problem, such as a modernization or expansion program, new sales plans, or a new training program. Or you may schedule a speaker who can help instill a sense of camaraderie in the conference participants.

Begin by asking what subjects or topics should be considered, and to what degree of depth. Then ask whether someone inside the company or outside can best accomplish your aim.

Be sure you consider the potential speaker's background and credentials very carefully. But don't depend on just his record alone. Many people with outstanding records are mediocre speakers. Ask other sources about the person's presentation skills.

The theme or topic you assign must be well suited to the speaker. It should be one he has knowledge about and interest in.

It should also be suitable for the audience. Before you make any final choices about a speaker or topic, analyze your audience. Think about topics that will gain their attention, balancing familiar information with the brand new. Many suggestions for choosing both a topic and a speaker are presented in Part II.

Be sure that the speaker or speakers are well briefed about what is expected of them, especially time limits. The following checklist is useful for your program committee:

1. Do all affected departments and individuals know who the speakers are and what their topics will be?

2. Do you have the materials about them you will need for publicity purposes, i.e., biographies and photos?

3. Who will introduce them?

4. Must arrangements be made for their lodging and meals?

5. Will they be picked up at an airport, etc., and by whom?

6. What company officials should greet or be introduced to them?

7. If they're giving a lecture, will they take questions afterward?

8. What about site arrangements, i.e., rostrum, sound system, projectors, props, water and glasses?

9. Are there any bells or phones at the program site that could ring during the presentation? (Make arrangements to turn them off.)

10. Have arrangements been made to make prompt payments?

You should consider preparing a memo for each speaker. Outline his or her entire schedule, including transportation arrangements, meals, and social functions. List lodging arrangements and procedures to be followed at motels or hotels if the company is paying for accommodations. Profile the audience the speaker will be addressing, including estimates of size.

Where to Hold Your Conference

Very early in the planning process, you should decide whether the event will be held on company premises or elsewhere. Note: The ideal setting for your annual stockholders' meeting probably won't be appropriate for an executive conference on company policy and vice versa. Also, if you've always held meetings or conferences at a certain site, it may be time to change.

Actual site selection probably will be best handled by a committee appointed for that task. It should make on-site inspections, negotiate with caterers and convention sales managers, etc.

Before the committee can begin its work, you will have to consider the following:

1. Type of place required
   company auditorium
   company cafeteria or
   dining room,
   special functions
   room
   other company facility
   hotel (airport hotel?
   major hotel?
   resort hotel?
   foreign hotel?)
   convention hall
   club
   arena
   ship

2. Type of area
   country (mountains?
   seashore?)
   city
   abroad

3. Climate/season
   tropical
   temperate
   winter
   spring
   summer
   fall

4. Price range
   economical
   moderate
   expensive
   luxury

5. Image
   time-to-economize
   ultramodern
   old world
   traditional

Once you have a clear idea of the kind of setting you want, give your suggestions to the person or the committee charged with the responsibility for making a final choice and reserving space. The sooner this process begins, the better.

Timing Considerations

At this point, you will also need to prepare a list of preferred times and dates for your event. This is a necessary step before definite scheduling and site selection arrangements can be made. This checklist will help:

- day or days of the week (first choice, second choice, third choice)

- date or dates (first choice, second choice, third choice)

- arrival time (or time event will begin)

- departure time (or time event will end)

- conflicting events (pay special attention to other meetings being held in the same building and in the same location; note holidays, long weekend conflicts)

- convenience (check transportation schedules)

- registration cutoffs

Two hints from successful conference planners:

1. If non-company people are to be invited, or your potential audience is made up of commuters, avoid Mondays and Fridays. Wednesdays for evening events are generally inadvisable because many people plan to go elsewhere, like the theater.

2. Develop an overall time schedule for all pre-event activities, in-progress activities, and post-event activities—and allow for periodic checks on everything taking place elsewhere.

The Convention Liaison Manual, which is packed with inside tips and suggestions, includes a wealth of checklists that cover just about any eventuality you might come across in running a convention or major conference. Prepared by the editors of Successful Meetings Magazine in cooperation with the Convention Liaison Council's editorial committee, the book can be obtained from: Secretary, Convention Liaison Council. 1575 I Street, N.W., Washington, DC 20005.

GETTING DOWN
TO SPECIFICS ON
CONFERENCE SITE SELECTION

Geography and transportation are two key considerations in choosing a conference site. Select a place that is accessible to attendees in relation to the type of transportation the majority of them will be using. Here is a checklist of the things you should keep in mind:

- good transportation services available (frequent express nonstop flights in and out, etc.)

- airport nearby

- centrally or conveniently located

- adequate public transportation

- taxis readily available

- rental car services nearby

Sources to check in these areas include regional or city convention and visitors bureaus. They can provide you with information on the facilities available and will even arrange for an on-site visit to hotels, resorts, arenas, and so on.

Individual hotels and resorts are also conduits of information, as the following excerpt from the ten-page planning guide of the Denver, Colorado, Hilton hotel illustrates:

> Stapleton International Airport, the world's eighth busiest, is served by 14 airlines, putting it within easy reach of virtually every city in North America. Rail and bus service to Denver is also good, and since Denver lies at the junction of East-West Interstate 70 and North-South Interstate 25, it is also convenient to get to by automobile.

The guide also describes the location of the hotel in relation to the city's main shopping district, government buildings, financial district, and the airport.

HOTELS AND CONFERENCE CENTERS

In selecting a site, ask these questions:

- What is the best part of town?

- Is it readily accessible?

- What is the reputation of the hotel or conference center (for food, service, cooperation, etc.)?

- How well suited is the facility to the conference or meeting objectives?

- How well suited is it to the mood or atmosphere?

If you're booking a hotel or resort, inquire about the following:

- individual rates
- block rates
- dining and function space
- air conditioning or heating
- amount of exhibit space
- recreational facilities
- available manpower
- audio-visual facilities
- space for coffee breaks
- space for registration

Check on the other events scheduled for the hotel or center at the same time you'll be using it. Ask if there are events scheduled immediately preceding or following yours that would affect your plans. (Will there be enough staff available at all times? Will the rooms you need be free when you need them?)

Audio-Visual Services

You will also want to check out audio-visual services. Hotels and convention centers should be able to provide you with a list that resembles Exhibit 10, which was supplied by a major U.S. hotel.

EXHIBIT 10.

Sample audio-visual equipment checklist

**General Information
Relating to Electrical Services Available**

Mikes

Mezzanine	Colorado	1 mike jack	4 mikes can be handled
Rooms:	Silver	1 mike jack	4 mikes can be handled
	Gold	1 mike jack	4 mikes can be handled
	Century	1 mike jack	4 mikes can be handled
	Spruce	1 mike jack	4 mikes can be handled
	Denver	1 mike jack	4 mikes can be handled

The above rooms receive one mike at no charge. Additional mikes at $15.00 per day. All the above are sufficiently small enough to not normally require a mike.

Grand Ballroom: Any number of mikes can be installed; 2 complimentary. $15.00 per day for each mike over two.

Junior Ballroom: Same as Grand Ballroom, both in numbers and charges.

Grand & Junior Ballrooms, combined: Same as Grand Ball Room and Junior Ball Room, both in number and charges (Two at no charge).

Assembly Room 1: One mike jack; one complimentary mike. $15.00 per day for each additional mike.

Assembly Room 2: Same as Assembly 1.

Assembly Room 3: Same as Assembly 1.

Assemblies, combined: Refer to above.

Empire Room: Five mike jacks. Two complimentary mikes. $15.00 per day for each additional mike.

Mikes

Empire Lounge: Two mike jacks. One mike complimentary. $15.00 per day for each additional mike.

Empire Room & Lounge, combined: Two complimentary mikes. $15.00 per day for each additional mike.

Savoy Room: No mike inputs. $75.00 charge per day for portable unit.

Empire Hall: No mike inputs.

Empire Foyer: Two mike inputs. One complimentary mike. $15.00 per day for each additional mike.

Note: Paging system may be set up in any part of the Empire Level but mike should be located at specific areas, thus advice from soundman is necessitated.

Beverly Room: Two mike inputs; one complimentary mike. $15.00 per day for each additional mike.

Biltmore Room: No mike inputs. None required because of size.

Vail Room: Two mike inputs; one complimentary mike. $15.00 per day for each additional mike.

Breckenridge Room: Three mike inputs. One complimentary mike. $15.00 per day for each additional mike.

Terrace Room: Two mike inputs; one complimentary mike. $15.00 per day for each additional mike.

Note: A mike should not be installed in Terrace Room that is used simultaneously as a meeting in the Empire Room because of sound carryover to Empire Room. Ceiling design is factor.

Terrace Foyer: Two mike inputs; one complimentary mike. $15.00 per day for each additional mike.

Mikes

Note: The Terrace Foyer is capable of being divided into two sections by means of portable air walls. When this is accomplished, one of the rooms is without its own private sound system. A portable system can be implemented at a fee of $75.00 per day.

Convention Lobby: A mike can be installed but it involves running a line from Assembly Room 1. This *must be accomplished* prior to the installation of any exhibit booths. A special charge of $15.00 plus labor charge of $20.00 will be assessed for a mike placed in the Convention Lobby.

Aspen, Birch, Cedar & Statler Rooms: Each is small enough not to require a mike, and jacks are not available.

Numbers and types of microphones available

2 Neck Mikes	2 630 Electrovoice
20 635 Electrovoice	10 Table mike stands
5 Floor mike stands	1 Piano boom stand

Sound equipment being used within the hotel is Bogan and Altec Lancing. Mike inputs are *all* low impedance.

When a soundman is required to "stand by" and monitor a system, a charge of $20.00 per hour with a three-hour minimum shall apply. If tape recording equipment is desired it can be rented on behalf of a client; hotel has no recording system.

Note: Whenever an electrician/soundman is required to work directly with a meeting (stand by), providing assistance with sound, lighting, TV, etc., a minimum charge of three hours at $20.00 per hour shall apply.

Spotlights and House Lights

2100 watt incandescent follow spots. One spot and operator at $60.00 for the first three hours, $20.00 for each additional hour or part thereof.

2100 watt stationary spot—$35.00 per day.

150 to 500 watt stationary spot—$15.00 per day each.

750 watt stationary spot—$20.00 per day each.

Because of the design of the hotel, certain areas must have the interior lighting controlled by an electrician (Grand Ballroom, Junior Ballroom, Assembly Rooms 1, 2 & 3). The charge for this stand-by service is $20.00 for each hour with a three-hour minimum. However, one man can control each of the above areas simultaneously.

The floor lighting in the Empire Room can be controlled by client. Should client desire on/off service on the chandeliers in Empire Room, a stand-by electrician will be necessitated and the fee noted above shall apply.

All remaining meeting space not identified in the two prior paragraphs has control switches either in the room or just outside the door and can be operated by client.

Footstage Lighting: $21.00 charge plus $20.00 per hour installation fee.

Backstage Lighting: Four banks of colored lights—red, blue and amber. $21.00 charge plus $20.00 per hour installation fee.

Frontstage Lighting: Three banks of white—$35.00 charge plus $20.00 per hour installation fee.

Should an electrician be required to change colors continuously, or periodically, an additional charge of $20.00 per hour is required.

Intercom System (2-way): $20.00 per headset (8 available).

TV and Closed-Circuit TV

TV sets can be installed in any of the following rooms: Grand & Junior Ballrooms, Assemblies 1, 2 & 3; Colorado, Silver, Gold, Century, Spruce, Denver Rooms; in the Convention Lobby (Rabbit ears).

Meeting rooms from ground level down do not have TV facilities; an antenna can be placed on the roof of a nearby office building and service fed into the area. A fee of $20.00 per hour, plus materials will apply.

Rental fees for TV sets as follows: $55.00 per day for each color set. If setup is unusual in nature a $20.00 per hour labor charge shall apply.

The hotel does have closed-circuit facilities but does not have cameras of R.F. generators and this must be ordered a minimum of one week in advance. $20.00 per hour fee shall apply for installation, dismantling, etc.

Closed-circuit TV can be installed from Grand Ballroom Complex to the Empire Room by using one zoom lens camera and one closed-circuit TV projector projected on a 10' screen for the sum of approximately $810.00. This covers a four-hour time period; for longer periods the cost would be higher due to technician operating time. *One week notice required* to arrange for closed-circuit services.

SPECIAL NOTE: No electrical service will be installed until the hotel electrician has a signed work order in his hands.

Electrical Service Available:	Service Rate:	
	120 volt service	
120 volt, A.C. Single phase	0 to 800 watts	$15.00
208 volt, A.C. Single phase	800 to 1000 watts	20.00
208 volt, A.C. Three phase	1000 to 1500 watts	25.00
	1500 to 2000 watts	30.00
	2000 to 3000 watts	40.00
	over 3000	$2.00 per 100 watts

General Conditions:

All electrical connections must be ordered in advance or by contacting our representative in the hotel. Orders received in advance will be installed first.

All electrical connections must be made by hotel electricians. Any type of multiple connections such as twin sockets, cube taps, etc., *will not* be permitted. There shall not be over five connections to any one circuit. The exhibitors' electrical equipment must be properly wired and meet the Fire Underwriters approval.

Rates quoted for electrical connections cover only the bringing of service to a booth in the most convenient manner and does not include connecting equipment, special wiring or repairs to exhibitors' equipment. This will be done on a time-and-material basis.

All hotel material and equipment is furnished on a rental basis, and remains the property of the hotel. **Exhibitors will be charged the retail price plus 50% for all items not returned.**

Service Rate:

or 120 volt service

each 15 amp circuit	25.00
each 20 amp circuit	30.00
each 30 amp circuit	40.00
over 30 amp circuit (per amp)	2.50

208 volts single-phase service

each 15 amp circuit	27.00
each 20 amp circuit	40.50
each 30 amp circuit	54.00
each 40 amp circuit	67.50
each 50 amp circuit	81.00
each 60 amp circuit	94.50

208 volts three-phase service

each 15 amp circuit	30.00
each 20 amp circuit	45.00
each 30 amp circuit	60.00
each 40 amp circuit	72.00
each 50 amp circuit	85.00
each 60 amp circuit	100.00
each 100 amp circuit	175.00

Spotlights

All spotlights (ceiling, floor stand, or clamp-on) each: $15.00. Follow spot & operator (min. 3 hrs.): $75.00.

Motor Connections
120 volt single phase:

All motors will be connected on a time-and-material basis.

Labor Rates:
Electricians, carpenters, and plumbers: $20.00 per hour

General Conditions:

All orders requiring over 10,000 watts of 120 volt or 208 volt single-phase, and all 208 volt three-phase current, must be received 7 days prior to setup. If these large orders are received any later, the rates quoted may not apply, and service will be installed on a time-and-material basis.

Any service ordered over and above a 20 amp 120V:

Should your equipment or exhibit not require service or doesn't arrive at this location, you will still be charged ½ of normal charge.

Labor Rates:

All holidays are worked at double time rate.

A charge of $75.00 per day shall apply to any portable sound system needed for areas without hotel sound equipment.

See other side for Order Blank Price subject to change without notice.

Meeting Location Contacts

Seasoned conference planners stress the importance of meeting the people with whom you'll be working should your event be held at a hotel or similar facility. Ask to meet:

- hotel or resort manager
- convention manager
- convention salesmen
- banquet manager and caterer

- service manager
- maître d'hôtel
- bell captain

Ask the convention manager or salesperson to show you the meeting and function rooms you will be using. Also look at some typical sleeping rooms.

One professional tip: Ask to see single as well as double sleeping rooms. Also ask to see the smallest single rooms that might be assigned to guests. Some hotels have spacious double rooms but barely adequate single rooms in terms of size and appointments.

EXHIBITS AND FREIGHT ARRANGEMENTS

This area is often neglected by first-time conference planners. Here is a checklist that will help you avoid problems in this regard:

- obtain plan of exhibit area

- note ceiling height

- check figures on how much weight floors can sustain

- find out whether floor space is on one level, flat, or if there are variations

- see if there are problems with noise

- look for storage facilities

- examine elevators and ramps to exhibit area

- check out the costs of packing/unpacking and setting up exhibits if this is done by hotel or conference center personnel

- when exhibits can be set up, taken down

SECURITY

Don't take security for granted. Discuss this matter during your negotiations with a facility's liaison person or the convention manager. Here are some questions you should be sure to ask:

1. Is security a problem in the vicinity of the hotel or conference center?

2. Is security a problem in the hotel? If so, what precautions has the management taken to resolve the problem? (For example, are there extra guards on duty after dark and locked entrances and exits?)

3. Is there a special entrance/exit for special guests?

LICENSES AND RESTRICTIONS

It's also a good idea to check in advance about any "house rules" or legal requirements that may restrict what your group wants to do. Inquire about union regulations. Example: Must a member of the electrician's union be present when audio-visual equipment is used. If so, will you be charged?

Liquor

Be especially careful about liquor licensing and serving policies. Many hotels and resorts require that liquor served on the premises be purchased and served through their caterer. Some hotels demand that you hire a bartender and rent a room for every reception.

Note: It's a good idea to keep a record of the beer and liquor consumed by your conference attendees. This will help you keep track of charges. Plus, you'll have a guide you can consult in the future. If you're uncertain about the proper amounts to order, the hotel or conference center banquet manager can help.

Food Arrangements

Keep conference objectives and themes in mind, and food and beverage arrangements will follow naturally. Just ask the basics:

What to serve? Where to serve it? When to serve it? Who is to serve it? How to serve it (sit-down functions, buffet, etc.)?

When you discuss these questions with the banquet manager before you sign a contract, be sure to ask for total price agreements.

CONTRACTS AND AGREEMENTS

After you have decided on a specific date and site, you are ready to sign an agreement. This contract should spell out in detail the obligations of both the hotel or conference center and your company.

Prepare Special Directions and Instructions

You should forward precise information about your needs to the hotel. Be sure this information arrives well in advance of your event.

EXHIBIT 11.

Sample letter outlining convention needs

<hr/>

The Starrs Company
Woodland Road
Pittsburgh, Pennsylvania 15232

March 1, 19—

Mr. John J. Chambers
Director of Sales
Main Lakes Conference Center
Greensburg, PA 15601

Dear Mr. Chambers:

Enclosed please find setup directions for all our group meetings, setup directions for our special functions (exhibits, registration, the president's address, evening receptions, and
workshops), and a list of the rooms we want reserved for our
planning committee.

Registration

Location: Founders Foyer
Time: 5 pm to 10 pm, Thursday, April 24
                9 am to 3 pm, Friday, April 25

Setup: We need 1 large rectangular table with 5
                chairs, water pitcher, ashtrays, and
                wastebaskets for registration. There should
                be a large bulletin board for thumbtacked
                messages, several easels for registration
                signs, and an in-house phone in the
                registration area.

                We will need a small locked office near the
                foyer to store registration materials prior to
                the opening of registration and in the
                evening after registration is closed.

President's Address

Location:	Auditorium
Time:	8:15 pm to 9:30 pm, Saturday, April 26

Setup: There should be a raised speaker's platform with a head table, two chairs, a table podium and microphone, and a water station. We are making arrangements to provide the speaker with an overhead projector and screen, the screen to be placed behind the speaker. In front of the speaker should be placed 200–225 chairs, theater style, which can be folded up and removed immediately following his speech, to make way for the cocktail party, which will take place in the same room.

Evening Reception

Location:	Auditorium and Reception Room
Time:	9:30 pm to 12 midnight, Saturday, April 26

Setup: This will be an open bar. Arrangements are being made through Catering. This party is to begin immediately following the president's address and will involve the removal of the chairs that have been set up for the address.

Mason

Time: 8 am to 5 pm, Thursday, April 24
8 am to 5 pm, Friday, April 25
8 am to 5 pm, Saturday, April 26
8 am to 5 pm, Sunday, April 27

NOTE: This room will be needed on a 24-hour basis even though it will be open only during the day.

Setup: We will need 12 bulletin boards, 4 large rectangular tables, each large enough to seat 8 people, 20 extra chairs, ashtrays, ice water, wastebaskets, and an in-house phone. We would also like to have an easel placed outside the Mason Room.

Woodward

Time: Same as above
NOTE: This room will also be needed on a 24-hour basis.

Setup: We will need 7 or 8 card tables, with 4 chairs per table, ice water, ashtrays, wastebaskets, and an in-house phone.

Exhibits

Location: Founders Room
Time: 1 pm to 5 pm, Thursday, April 24, setup
8 am to 5 pm, Friday, April 25, setup and exhibit
9 am to 5 pm, Saturday, April 26, exhibit
9 am to 5 pm, Sunday, April 27, exhibit
5 pm Sunday, April 27, dismantling

Setup: We now have 17 exhibits with a total of 26 tables. Rectangular 6' × 8' tables should be set up with tablecloths and two chairs each. We are working on a chart showing placement of the exhibit tables, and I'll send this chart to you as soon as I receive it. This chart will show the exact tables to which Main Lakes personnel are to deliver the exhibits sent to the hotel. The exhibits should be in place at the proper tables by 1 pm on Thursday, April 24.

We would like to have an easel located at the main entrance to the Founders Room so that we may direct our guests to the exhibits.

As a security precaution, we request that the locks be changed on the doors to the Founders Room, and that a single key be made up for the new locks. (Please let me know what it will cost to have this done.)

We would like to have a continental breakfast set up in the Founders Room for our exhibitors on Friday morning, April 25, at 8 am. This breakfast should be charged to our master account. Joe Callanan, my assistant, will contact the catering director about this.

I'll give you a call on Monday, April 7, to discuss any last-minute arrangements. Michael McKinsey, Walt Anderson, and I will arrive to attend a preconference meeting on Wednesday, April 23. Will you please schedule a time and place for this meeting, and confirm our reservations for that evening?

Looking forward to working with you at Main Lakes.

Sincerely,

Samuel J. Nichols

Financial Arrangements

Decide in advance how much money you are prepared to spend on the event and stick to that budget. After you've estimated overall cost, add an additional 10% to be safe.

Here is a checklist of costs to consider when drawing up your budget:

personnel	exhibit	transportation
sleeping room	phone	equipment
meeting room	meals/food	entertainment

gifts	speaker(s) fee(s)	mailing
security	insurance	gratuities
taxes		

Tip: For future reference, note each individual event and the costs associated with it.

Foreign Meetings

If your meeting is to be held abroad, or if you will have attendees from other countries, you will want to pay attention to these details.

- Send passport and visa information to all parties concerned.

- Send conference materials, information on special regulations, money, transportation, and accommodations to attendees.

- Check on whether you will need simultaneous or sequential translation during the conference.

- Check facilities for simultaneous translations. Be sure interpreters are available.

- Check on the need for foreign language copies of papers, reports.

Remember: Hotels and conference centers abroad are just as happy to send you information about their facilities as hotels and centers in your own country. Here's an ad placed in American newspapers by an international convention center:

We've got a theatre for movies...a stage, a banquet hall...cultural halls...assembly halls for private business meetings, executive suites for board of directors' meetings, a coffee shop and restaurants...and arcades for trade and art exhibits. (We have) 18 meeting rooms seating 50 to 5,000, 7-language simultaneous interpretation system, sophisticated technical and electronic equipment, a full range of ancillary services, and a...staff of experienced, skilled and eager-to-please coordinators.

For inquiries, please contact our Operations Department.

ANTICIPATING UNFORESEEN DIFFICULTIES

Your featured speaker is delayed or cancels at the last moment. The public-address system or mike breaks down just as the conference begins. More or fewer people show up than you expected.

What do you do? You're in trouble if you don't anticipate problems in advance, a key component of your pre-event planning. Decide what you'll do if the main speaker can't make it. Have a backup person in mind.

Do you want to have a teleconference screen and telephone set up so the original speaker can make his talk in that fashion? Pre-think emergencies. It's the very best way to avoid them.

Put yourself through as many disaster situations as you can conjure up. Think through the event from pre-registration to post-adjournment, considering each step, each program, each arrangement. Try to think of the difficulties each attendee might encounter and the information he or she will need before, during, and after the conference.

Of course, there will probably be some problems you couldn't possibly anticipate. Just keep moving forward as best you can.

AFTER THE EVENT

As soon as possible following your event, poll the attendees to see why they feel the event was a success or not. Meet with those who helped to plan and implement the conference, and record their ideas and opinions in a detailed memo.

It's also a good idea to sit down and talk with the banquet manager, conference center manager, and anyone else with whom you've worked closely. Get their feedback. And review your final bills very carefully.

Finally—relax and take a few days off. You deserve it.

EFFECTIVE
ARRANGEMENTS FOR ALL
BUSINESS MEETINGS

In planning small meetings and large, it's important to take into consideration the physical circumstances—room size and seating arrangements in particular.

CHOOSING THE RIGHT ROOM

The size of your meeting should guide your choice of where to hold it. Ten people in an auditorium will feel intimidated by the empty space. Sounds echo, and hearing is difficult because voices are not contained and reflected properly. On the other hand, a small office may make the same ten people feel crushed. The room gets hot and stuffy, the easy interchange of talk becomes inhibited by the discomfort members feel in the claustrophobic atmosphere.

Be sure to try to choose a room that fits your group. In most circumstances you will have to make concessions. Only certain rooms will be available when you need them.

Of course, once you become chairman of the board, you won't have to worry about room availability.

If you are forced to make a choice between a large room and small, think about the effect you want to create. A little crowding (if not extremely uncomfortable) may even help engender a sense of community and purpose. Minor distractions can initiate relationships if participants don't know one another well.

The British House of Commons was intentionally designed to hold only two-thirds of its membership. That is usually all that shows up, so the room doesn't seem empty. For the occasional crisis session, the crowding heightens the feeling of urgency.

Often you can make an overly large room suitable for a small meeting by partitioning one corner. For instance, when your staff of ten meets in the company cafeteria, you can create a sense of comfort, yet isolation, with movable partitions.

ARRANGING SEATS AND TABLES

In small meetings—fifteen people or less—the seating pattern makes an important difference. "A human being is a source of energy," claims psychologist Harry Levinson, a Harvard University industrial consultant, "and most of it radiates in the direction he or she is facing."

According to one school of thought, this "source of energy" theory militates against the round-table meeting. Proponents claim that several sources of energy distributed evenly around a circle facing inward cancel each other out.

Thus the energy of ten people at a round table is directed back at the participants. It's locked in and doesn't add up to anything. In the same sense, the long oval conference table focuses each person's energy on the person opposite, thereby critically restricting it.

When everyone faces the person at the end of the table, the collective energy is aimed at that one individual, not at the common problem. Of course, many managers enjoy being the focus of attention. That arrangement works better for formal presentations and report meetings, but it often inhibits easy collaboration.

Don't reject the round table, though, if you're looking for a more casual, opinion-oriented discussion. It's like sitting around after dinner. The closed form encourages a heightened mood. Usually this mood is convivial.

But sometimes the same arrangement encourages and exacerbates anger and aggression, if these emotions happen to be present. In the circular setting, negative emotions will be aimed directly at individuals and can lead to heated encounters.

"If you want an intense face-to-face exchange, the round table is ideal," said Michael Doyle and David Straus, of Interaction Associates, a San Francisco consulting firm specializing in business meetings. "But if you want a problem-focused meeting, sitting around the table doesn't work very well."

The Advantages of the Semicircle

Doyle and Straus agree with behavioral scientists that the best way for meeting participants to be seated is in a semicircle facing the leader.

Two factors govern how a semicircle is set up: the location of the doors and the location of a wall suitable for blackboard notes or space for a flip chart.

Ideally, the semicircle should face away from the door, so that people coming and going will not disrupt the meeting. If the door is in the line of vision of the participants, all eyes will instinctively follow interruptions.

Consider Your Meeting's Atmosphere

There is almost universal agreement that the physical environment has a significant effect on the psychological environment. Formal settings induce formality. This may be appropriate for the announcement of an important decision, the signing of a contract, or the promotion of a top executive. But formal settings are not conducive to getting down to real detail work. For such sessions, you need an informal space where you can push chairs together, hang papers on the wall, and generally act and react in comfort.

Studies by Harvard's Levinson and other psychologists show that, for groups as well as individuals, a formal atmosphere inhibits the mood of "relaxed concentration" necessary for the most productive work. Leaders usually get their best results when the participants feel comfortable in their surroundings. A reasonably attractive office may well be more suitable for most meetings than a formal conference room. The informality of any session, of course, must be balanced by a focused and organized meeting environment, with as few interruptions and distractions as possible. You should become sensitive to this balance, so that you will know when to relax and when to push for more work.

Making Presentations

Most meetings depend to a great degree on presentations. Before the group tackles the creative or problem-solving assignment, it must absorb the relevant facts and figures, the insights and observations of the leader and those with special knowledge.

One way to develop a presentation is to approach the situation in much the same way that you analyze and design a meeting. Ask yourself the traditional planning questions: who, why, what, when, where, how, and how many?

Who is Your Audience?

A good place to start your presentation planning is with a consideration of your audience. Ask yourself:

- Who are these people?

- What are their expectations from my presentation?

- What do they want and need to know?

- How much do they already know about my subject?

- Do they understand the jargon or should I translate for a general audience?

- What level of detail shall I present—very specific, very general?

- What will my audience do with the information?

- What does the audience know about me?

Chapter 9 explores audience analysis in greater depth.

CHOOSING MATERIAL FOR PRESENTATION

Many presentations bore the audience because they contain too much information. People can retain only so much. Give much thought to what is really essential. Pick out a few key ideas—and stress those. Leave the background information for review in printed material accompanying your talk.

Here's a tip: Send your written material, along with your agenda, to the participants ahead of time or hand it out at the end of the meeting, not at the beginning. People will just concentrate on what they see in their hands and you will have lost your audience. Only use reference material if you need to lead people through technical or financial data or to get feedback and criticism on what you've written.

Some other considerations:

- How much time should your presentation take?

- How much time should you use for questions?

- Do you need to sharpen your presentation with visuals?

- What immediate impact will your presentation have on the audience?

Remember: If your presentation is going to take more than half an hour, consider giving *two* presentations at separate times, if that's feasible, or incorporating a break into the session.

GUIDELINES FOR VISUAL PRESENTATIONS

According to research by the 3M Corporation, people retain only 10% of what they hear in a presentation and 20% of what they see. But they retain 50% of what they hear *and* see.

Bert Y. Auger, a 3M consultant, offers a list you can use in preparing your visual presentation.

1. Build your chart or transparency around ideas, not trick displays. Remember, your visuals can never be better than the thought they present.

2. Try to identify the main points you want to convey, both from your vantage point and that of the audience. Then choose the type of chart or graph accordingly.

3. Work out a presentation script, a narrative outline of what you propose to say. As you develop it, keep in mind the visuals you intend to use.

4. Ask yourself these basic questions about the visuals:

   • Are they simple, concise, understandable, believable and authoritative?

   • Are they organized in sequence to reach a logical conclusion?

   • Are they directed to the special interests of those to whom you are speaking?

   • Do they most effectively help you reach your objectives?

   • Do you have too many, or too few?

   • If you were the audience, would you be convinced by them?

5. Keep in mind that general theories, principles, and rules are hard to absorb. The tangible is always preferable to the abstract. Examples, anecdotes, experiences, and problems that are familiar to the audience will be the most effective.

6. A little humor in good taste can relieve audience tension and emphasize a point. But sound judgment is impor-

tant. Avoid making members of the audience the subjects of your joking. If there is any doubt as to inducing
offense or embarrassment, drop the idea.

Chapter 14 in Part II offers more suggestions for visual
presentations.

Preparing Visual Aids

There are three rules that will guide you through the preparation of most visuals. These rules are based on how much
the mind can readily grasp and absorb before moving on to
the next mental stimulus. They are:

1. One point or relationship per visual.
2. Maximum of six or seven words per line.
3. Maximum of six or seven lines per visual.

The dominance of the single idea should be stressed.
You want to concentrate the thought of the entire audience
on one theme, one idea, one formula, or one key fact before
you move ahead. If the audience gets nothing else from a
particular visual, you must make it grasp the main point.

If you want your ideas to be understood, use arguments
and examples that build on the familiar. Appeal to the interests and motivations of your individual audience members.

Make up some rough drafts of the visual projections
and view them from the most distant seat. If you can't read
the print, use larger letters, even though this means elimi-
nating some material or using an additional chart. As a rule,
the smallest letters should be about three inches high when
projected.

Some charts consist of several lines of reading matter. You can give emphasis by combining words, diagrams, pictures, and symbols.

Create a center of interest through physical arrangement of the materials and use of color. If you do not use color, vary the heaviness of lines or in some other way contrast light and dark. Emphasis can also be achieved by the relative size of individual lines and figures.

Simplicity is another rule. Maintain the one-main-idea concept. Every visual should be crisp, dynamic, and short; the text should be tight and bright. Every unnecessary or questionable item should be eliminated. If you have a choice of two equally strong words, use the shorter of the two. Use bold lines and forms; avoid fine scale. Cartoons and other artwork can be powerful additions, but don't risk diverting the viewer's focus from the main idea.

THE MEETINGS OF TOMORROW

There's much talk these days about the "office of the future." No aspect of modern life is immune to the onrush of computer technology's latest tools. Meetings are no exception. Thus the birth of teleconferencing.

Teleconferencing is an area that many large companies are beginning to investigate as a cost-effective alternative to traditional conferences. By using either video or audio measures or both, you can hook together a variety of locations as if everyone were in the same room.

Many companies are climbing on the teleconferencing bandwagon. Atlantic Richfield Company (ARCO), the oil giant, developed a complete $20 million teleconferencing network in Los Angeles. The network enables key executives to confer with one another visually by use of a satellite hookup and wall-sized projection screens. The regular weekly meetings of the company no longer require executives to fly to Los Angeles from all over the country. Instead, they walked into a room near their office equipped with tele-conferencing equipment.

A Wide Range of Video Alternatives

Although the video aspect of teleconferencing has been technically feasible for some time, the new technology has made it easier and cheaper than ever before.

There are legions of video consulting firms in major cities that provide expert service for setting up your own videoconferences. There is even an international association for teleconferencing called (aptly) International Teleconferencing Association, 1299 Woodside Dr., Suite 101, McLean, VA 22102.

One recent major development is the entry of large hotel-motel chains in the videoconferencing market. Holiday Inns Incorporated used its own facilities to reach 16,000 employees around the world last year. It beamed a 90-minute program, part live and part taped, to 131 locations in the United States, Hong Kong, Frankfort, and London. That videocast also reached customers, stockholders, financial analysts, and media representatives. Total cost was $75,000, only about $5 per person. Holiday Inn has some 336 permanent hand-wired locations in 42 states. Marriot planned to have 60 in place by 1984 and Hyatt anticipated 25 by early in the year.

The two main considerations you have to address in videoconferencing on this scale are the appropriateness of the medium and the cost.

Dealing with Teleconferences

In your current position, 3-way telephone hookups may be the extent of your teleconferencing. But if someday video-conferencing becomes a part of your job, you may have to deal with one or more of those chains. The services they provide include:

- a schedule of all the locations you select

- meeting rooms

- guest rooms

- origination from local TV station, your office, even a plant or factory floor

- professional consultants for scriptwriting, coaching, graphics production and direction

- help in prerecording portions of the program

- food, beverage, and party arrangements

- host and hostesses

- help in devising themes, decoration, set up

- a direct-mail promotion program

Keep in mind one thing. No matter how simple or complicated your teleconferencing process is going to be, all the techniques proposed in this book for planning, writing an agenda, and so on are part and parcel of a successful endeavor.

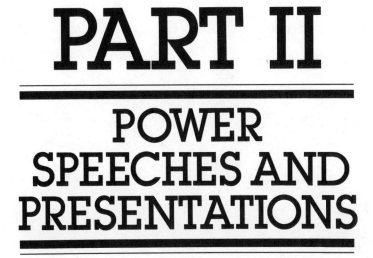

PART II

POWER SPEECHES AND PRESENTATIONS

Now that you've learned everything you've always wanted to know about meetings but were afraid to ask, it's time to turn to speeches and presentations.

Remember that many of the suggestions offered in Part I can be used as the foundation for understanding and practicing what you'll find in Part II, and vice versa.

Whether you're currently a good speaker, a run-of-the-mill speaker, or no speaker at all—you'll add power and polish to every thought you express by incorporating the suggestions in this section into your verbal activities.

When you are called on to make an important business presentation, when a community group asks you to be its guest speaker, when a reporter sets up an interview with you, whenever a speaking opportunity presents itself—the material in this part will give you the resources to project your best possible spoken image.

FIVE INGREDIENTS
FOR SUCCESS IN SPEAKING

The secret of effective public speaking—at a meeting of three people, a congregation of thirty, or a conference of 300—is remarkably simple. Be yourself!

"But," you may object, "that's not so easy."

"Maybe not. But it's certainly a lot easier than trying to be somebody else!"

That's the reply you will hear from the experts, including Dennis Becker, president of the Speech Improvement Company of Brookline, Massachusetts. Becker is one of a growing number of specialists who help business people become effective public speakers. His role, he says, is simply to teach his clients the techniques of being themselves. "Being yourself," Becker says, "means being at your best. I don't teach rhetoric, eloquence, or tricks. I teach sincerity, consideration for your audience, and simple clarity in the expression of ideas. It has been proven time and again that these are qualities that every business person can learn to project."

As the public's awareness of business heightens, the practices and techniques of specialists like Becker become increasingly important. Such "speech coaches" are busier than ever because business people—from CEO's to middle managers and every position in-between—are constantly being called upon to express their ideas and opinions at local meetings and luncheons of business associations, at national conferences and conventions, at seminars and educational gatherings, and on television forums and talk shows. In fact, the skills needed for success on those occasions also apply to the everyday matters of business—sales meetings, directors' meetings, talks to groups of employees, special in-company seminars and conferences, and so forth. "Formal speeches are only part of the picture," Becker contends. "Effectiveness in speaking carries over to practically every aspect of business. People who speak well are good communicators, and everybody knows how important that is."

Extensive research has revealed that there are basically five ingredients to success in public speaking that will help you display your best form in all your public appearances:

1. Poise and confidence

2. Sense of the audience and the occasion

3. Selection of material

4. Sense of the purpose of your talk

5. Delivery

POISE AND CONFIDENCE

Stage fright is a universal phenomenon. Nobody is totally immune, according to the experts. Such well-known speakers as Winston Churchill, Adlai Stevenson, and John Kennedy confessed to feeling nervousness and fear when facing audiences. Some have become so overwrought that they were physically ill. But all accomplished speakers have forced themselves to go on and have triumphed over their fears.

"Effective speakers make their nervousness work for them by directing it into appropriate channels," claims Raymond G. Smith, a former teacher of speech and theater at Indiana University. "Nervousness can be the spark that ignites your excitement and enthusiasm for the subject. It helps concentration. It's a source of energy."

Professor Smith recommends physical movement as a method for reducing tension and channeling nervous energy. "Move around the platform between ideas," he advises. "Gesture frequently. Walk to your charts, diagrams, or projections. Go through all the physical motions required in demonstrating or displaying models. Strive for dynamic bodily activity in every way you can."

Overcoming Nervousness

Paul Harrison, a popular speaker to groups of small business people in the northeastern United States, admits that he always gets "a nervous stomach" before appearing in public. "But I've learned how to conquer it," he said. "In fact, I've put together a pretty good system."

Harrison's approach for developing poise and confidence on a speaker's platform encompasses preparation for the talk as well as performance on the platform. Here are his suggestions:

- *Speak on a familiar topic.* Know your subject as thoroughly as possible. Do all the research necessary to make you confident that you know exactly what you're talking about.

- *Know your audience.* Find out what its members expect to hear from you. Check out their interests, occupations, age, and general knowledge of your subject area.

- *Organize.* A good talk is a purposeful entity, not just a collection of ideas and information. It should have an introduction, body, and conclusion. It should have a simple point, a purpose the audience clearly understands.

- *Practice.* Prepare an outline and deliver the talk out loud three or four times in private. Use a tape recorder and listen to the playback with as much objectivity as possible.

- *Make a conscious effort to relax.* The height of tension comes just before you're supposed to start. Take deep breaths, which help by increasing your supply of oxygen. Listen closely to the speaker who precedes you. You may become so interested that you forget your uneasiness.

- *Establish eye contact.* Look at your audience before you speak. This will draw its attention to you. Don't scan the audience every time you look up from your notes. Pick one person and deliver several words or phrases to him or her. Those sitting nearby will also feel you are speaking directly to them. Continue to look at individuals in other areas of the audience.

- *Be enthusiastic.* Usually the most important element in any successful talk is the speaker's enthusiasm, a quality that reflects other desirable qualities—believability and sincerity, among others.

- *Be brief.* A good speaker knows when to quit. Be aware of your time limit and stick to it. Remember: One of the most famous American speeches, President Lincoln's Gettysburg Address, used only 266 words.

- *Don't be too critical of yourself after the event.* Many veteran speakers half-jokingly claim that there are three speeches involved in any address: the one you thought you were going to give, the one you actually gave, and the one you delivered so brilliantly to yourself on the way home.

The late Dale Carnegie, famous for his positive-attitude approach to life, the man who helped thousands of business people discover the satisfactions and rewards of speaking in public, put it succinctly when he wrote: "The chief cause of your fear in public speaking is simply that you are unaccustomed to it. Practice, practice, practice!

"You will find, as thousands upon thousands have, that public speaking can *be made* a joy instead of an agony, merely by getting a record of successful speaking experiences behind you."

As you assume more responsibility at your company and achieve higher rank in the corporate structure, you'll find more opportunities coming your way for such practice.

Dressing the Part

Lee Bowman, former Hollywood actor/producer/director and speech consultant to Bethlehem Steel Corporation, stressed that your poise and confidence depend to some extent on the way you dress:

> You are trying to maintain the complete attention of your audience. But that attention should be riveted on your words,

not some peculiarity in the way you are dressed. So dress conservatively, whether male or female. Don't wear a loud tie or a sexy blouse. Don't have a bunch of pens sticking out of your breast pocket or a silk scarf around your neck. They are distracting and demoralizing, both to your audience and to you when facing their skeptical stares.

The short-sleeved summer shirt may be comfortable, but too much bare arm is devastating to a speaker's image. So is too much bare leg. Women shouldn't wear short or slit skirts and men should always wear above-the-calf socks.

The Right Perspective

Along with most veteran speakers who willingly discuss the topic, Barney Kingston emphasized preparation as the soundest way to overcome stage fright. "There is nothing that will give you a deeper sense of stage fright than not being properly prepared," he says.

Kingston, merchandising director for a sales magazine, recalled that it took more than preparation, though, to handle his first assignment to speak before a state convention:

> I thought I was ready for that major event. I spent two months on my subject, "Market Your Product the Direct Way." I practiced the talk before some friends, and they were enthusiastic. I was sure I was ready. A few hours before the main event, I walked into the huge armory where I would speak and saw hundreds of chairs, all spread out before the podium. I got stage fright, even though I was looking at an expanse of empty chairs! At that moment I hoped that an earthquake would hit the place so I wouldn't have to speak.
>
> Then I met the program chairman and told him my doubts. The chairman waved them aside. He told me that I was an expert at direct selling, that the audience had paid to hear me. "That's the important thing," he emphasized. "The peo-

ple have *paid* to hear what you have to say because you're an expert."

That simple statement gave Kingston an entirely new perspective.

"I was wondering what I was doing there, talking to those top-level executives," he said. "But once I got the right perspective my feelings switched from stage fright to exhilaration. Just think: hundreds of people paying just to hear me speak!"

Using Your Emotions

Poise and confidence come mainly from your basic attitudes about yourself, your audience, and what you can contribute to the occasion. Good attitudes can be developed, according to speech specialists. Again, your attitude reflects that original theme: Be yourself.

"The most effective speakers," Lee Bowman said, "are the people who have learned that public speaking is little more than private conversation—amplified. Most important of all, they have learned to overcome the schizophrenic tendency of most inexperienced speakers to assume entirely different personalities when they step up to the lectern."

Don't forget that a little stage fright is not a sign of incompetence. It's a perfectly normal reaction to a high-stress situation. It's a state of excitement generated by adrenalin-charged juices flowing through your body. Far from detracting from your performance, it can add to your effectiveness—provided you learn to channel it properly.

"Let your emotions show!" Bowman advised. "Don't stifle them. If you don't seem to be interested in what you're talking about, what can you expect from your audience? And when you let your excited inner feelings come to the surface, you're going to come through as someone who means what he is saying. You're going to be a more effective speaker."

SENSE OF THE AUDIENCE AND THE OCCASION

If you are a business person new to public speaking, it may surprise you to know that the typical invitation does not indicate what you are expected to talk about. Often it consists merely of a phone call from, for example, the program chairman of a local community organization. They'll say something like: "Hey, Jim, I hear you've done a lot of work on the impact of government regulations on plants along our river. We'd like to hear about it. How about giving a talk to our group next month at the regular Tuesday meeting on the 24th?"

Such an invitation leaves you with unanswered questions. You're sure to want to know how many club members have a direct interest in the subject. How many have enough technical knowledge about water pollution and government regulations to understand a detailed discussion on the subject? How many would respond to the subject if it were told in general terms, emphasizing the significance of what is happening but not going into much technical detail? How many come to meetings expecting to be entertained with jokes and stories?

These are fundamental questions that need to be answered before you begin to prepare your talk. For answers, probably the best source is the person who invites you. Ask him or her: Has your group heard other speakers on the same subject? Has your group organized a study or action committee on the subject? Why does the group want you to speak? Are there experts on the subject in the group?

Assessing Your Audience

Here are other considerations about your audience, formulated by Leon Fletcher, a former professor of speech at Monterey Peninsula College.

Attitude toward subject. Before you speak, determine whether or not your audience supports your point of view. If not definitely for it, are they against it, merely neutral, or able to be persuaded? The attitudes of your audience will affect your approach and presentation—not your point of view, just the manner of its presentation.

Attitude toward speaker. Will you have the audience's automatic respect? Will they believe you when you begin to talk? Or will you have to overcome some antagonism? For instance, if you're 5-foot-5 and weigh 200 pounds, you might have a little difficulty promoting an executives' physical-fitness program. But if you weighed 200 pounds six months ago and are now down to a trim 140 pounds, you would automatically command their attention.

Occupation. If your audience is made up of civil engineers, or local business people, or government legislators, or members of your industry's national association, you can build your speech on their common background. Mixed audiences, on the other hand, present added problems that must be considered in material selection and even manner of delivery.

Economic status.   It's important to know, at least in a general way, about the economic status of your audience, simply because economic status often affects attitudes on fundamental issues. The feelings of low-income individuals, for example, about government price controls are likely to be different from those of high-income groups. Such attitudes are often complex, conflicting, and surprisingly unpredictable. But it's wise to try to gauge your audience from an economic point of view so you'll have a surer feel for how to approach your subject.

Educational status.   Are the members of your audience mostly college graduates? High school graduates? Do they have about the same amount of education that you have? Substantially more? Or less? The answers will help determine to a large degree your language, examples, and emphasis. It's not a matter of changing your convictions or your point of view but of tailoring the level of your talk to your listeners.

Cultural status.   What publications does your audience like to read? Business publications? Newsweeklies? Trade or industry magazines? Newsletters? General interest magazines? Are they likely to be familiar with popular television programs? Will they understand references to recent industrial developments and new technologies? All are considerations to be kept in mind when writing your speech. You don't want to refer to events, trends, or ideas with which your audience is unfamiliar.

Sex.   An all-male audience? All female? Mixed? It makes a difference in how you approach your subject, your choice of anecdote and example, your emphasis, and even perhaps your choice of words.

Age. What range of ages might you expect in your audience? Here again, your approach at a junior achievement meeting at the local high school would be different from that at a national conference for the elderly.

The Motives of Your Audience

Then, you must consider your audience in terms of its motives and interests.

We are all controlled pretty much by the same basic desires. We want health, money, prestige, and love. If you can show an audience how to turn any *one* of these desires into reality, you're bound to succeed as a speaker.

If you can show that your talk is connected with health and longevity, your hearers will be extra-attentive. Self-preservation is a human instinct, and anything that relates to it is bound to interest an audience. A good topic for a local talk might be your company's after-hours fitness program for managers.

Professional, business, and social prestige can be as potent a motivation as health. The attractiveness of this appeal is reflected in the steady stream of magazine articles, television shows—and speeches—on the subject. "The Secret of Making People Like You," "How Not to Be Tongue-Tied at a Party," "Are You Being Promoted Right Over Your Head?" are just three titles of thousands that recur again and again in media. "How to Get Ahead" talks in any number of forms are almost always winners on the lecture circuit.

Caution: Don't try to give an "inspirational" talk of any kind, however, unless you truly believe in what you're saying and can support your assertions with sound and lively data, examples, and anecdotes. A flair for showmanship also helps, especially with sales people.

Any speech about economic security has much appeal. All business people are interested in ways of improving their operations, increasing sales and profits, and cutting costs. In fact, a subject such as "How to Beat Rising Prices" is almost universal these days, appealing not only to business people but to housewives, students, and just about every other kind of audience as well.

Rising to the Occasion

It is important to consider the kind of speech expected of you in terms of the occasion. This affects your tone and mood. The talk you give at a sales meeting in your own company would be vastly different from the one you give at the annual dinner honoring a member of local government.

Often the physical size and seating arrangements of the auditorium or room determine the formality of the occasion. The decorations, lighting, and special guests are equally important. Even the time of day—morning, afternoon, or evening—must be considered. The length and type of program, the objectives and accomplishments of the organization, whether your talk is the main event or only part of a larger program—all these factors have a bearing on how your audience will react.

Before every speech, ask yourself:

- What do my listeners want to hear?

- What do they believe will be good for them to hear?

- What do they want their friends and fellow listeners to hear?

On some occasions, your answers to these questions may not be wholly in line with what you want to tell this

EXHIBIT 12.

Audience analysis audit

Fill in the blanks or circle the most descriptive terms.

Audience/Group_____

1. Identify the objectives in addressing THIS audience. What do you want to happen as a result of it?

    _____
    _____
    _____

Keep these objectives in mind as you consider the items below.

2. SPECIFIC ANALYSIS of members of this audience—
    a. Their knowledge of the subject:
       High level   General   Limited   None
       Unknown
    b. Their opinions about the subject and/or the speaker or organization represented:
       Very favorable   Favorable   Neutral
       Slightly hostile   Very hostile   Unknown
    c. Their reasons for attending this event:_____

       _____
       _____
       _____

    d. Advantages and disadvantages of the speech's objectives to them as individuals:
       Advantages _____

       _____
       _____
       _____

       Disadvantages_____

       _____
       _____
       _____

3. GENERAL ANALYSIS of members of this audience—
    a. Their occupational relationships to the speaker and to
        your company:
        Customer   Top management
        Immediate management
        Peers   Subordinates   Other management
        Other workers   Public (local to facility or otherwise)
    b. Their familiarity with your company's business
        activities:
        Very familiar   Moderately familiar
        Slightly familiar
    c. Their vocabulary understanding level, depending on
        subject of speech:
        Technical   Nontechnical   Generally high
                       Generally low   Unknown
    d. Open-mindness (willingness to accept ideas to be pre-
        sented)
        Eager   Open   Neutral
        Slightly resistant   Strongly resistant   Unknown

4. Information and Techniques—
    a. Information and techniques most likely to gain the at-
        tention of this audience:
        Highly technical information Statistical comparisons
        Cost figures   Anecdotes   Demonstrations   Other

        _____

        _____

    b. Information or techniques likely to get negative re-
        actions from this audience:

        _____

        _____

5. Summarize, in a few sentences, the most important infor-
    mation from the preceding four sections.

    _____

    _____

    _____

audience at this particular time. That will make your decision on how to handle the material more difficult. But whatever you do, you will be a more effective speaker if you have a clear idea of your audience and what they expect from you at that particular time.

Many speech professionals use checklists and forms that give a simple, direct method for analyzing audiences. Exhibit 12, an audience analysis audit, was prepared by the Bethlehem Steel Corporation.

SELECTING AND PREPARING YOUR MATERIAL FOR THE SPEECH

After you've analyzed your audience and the occasion of the talk, it's time to focus on your subject. "Be selective!" says John P. Guttenberg, Jr., former president of Guttenberg Associates, a Washington public-affairs consulting firm. "Choose your topic with care. It is an honor to be invited to speak, but it is of no value to be in the wrong place with the wrong topic. You probably have more latitude than you think in determining your topic or position in the program. Exercise it."

The truth is that even if the program chairman assigns a subject, you are almost always free to adapt that subject to your own preferences regarding what you select to talk about and how you do it.

Ask the following basic questions to help guide the selection process.

1. Do you have enough knowledge about the subject you're considering to provide the background for your speech?

("Knowledge" includes information you have gained from experience, conversation, thinking, and observing, as well as reading.)

2. Are you interested in the topic? If you are not, you can't expect the audience to be. A subject that interests you is much easier to talk about and will result in a better performance.

3. Are you sure the subject is suitable to your audience? Choose a subject that will gain attention—not one with which the audience is so familiar that it already knows all available information, and not one so far from its experience and its thinking that it has no interest. Respect your listeners' intelligence.

Choose Attention-Getting Subjects

What kinds of subjects gain the most attention? That's where your analysis of the audience assumes prime importance. Small business people will surely be interested in anything that affects the community in which they do business, in how they can make their businesses more profitable, and in national conditions that may have an impact on their work or their lives in one way or another.

Both the audience and the occasion suggest subjects for your talk. Often you'll be chosen to speak because you have special knowledge of a subject that a certain group finds interesting or important. Don't assume, though, that a group will be interested in a statistics-laden report because its members have asked you to talk on a technical subject. Chances are, they won't be. Look for interesting and entertaining ways of presenting every subject, no matter how "serious" or technical. You often can do this by examining your personal experiences, finding enlightening anecdotes or examples, and generally giving your talk a human touch.

If the choice of subject is entirely up to you, the first step, according to Orvin Larson of the Department of Speech and Theatre at Brooklyn College, is to ask yourself the following questions:

1. What am I really interested in?

2. What do I strongly believe?

3. What are my biggest complaints?

4. What are my strong likes?

5. What have I done, where have I been, whom have I known?

6. What have I seen or heard today?

"Such questions will uncover a wealth of attitudes, ideas, and facts. Do not ever think that you have nothing worth talking about," Larson said.

SENSE OF PURPOSE

Decide just what you want to accomplish with your speech. The general purposes of most successful speeches can be divided into five categories.

1. *Explain* a process, method, or theory.

2. *Inform* your audience about an event, person, policy, or institution.

3. *Convince* your audience of the truth or falsity of some idea, policy, or point of view.

4. *Arouse* your audience to action in regard to a cause.

5. *Entertain* your audience by revealing the humorous, sharing the exciting or the pleasant, or awakening its appreciation in the unusual and interesting.

Speech specialists recommend that you phrase your specific aim in a single sentence that states clearly and concisely exactly what you wish to accomplish in your speech. Examples:

- Adapt our direct mail techniques to your products and achieve a 15 percent gain in sales.

- The business people of this town should band together to help prevent crime in the streets.

- Price controls will not alleviate inflation; they'll increase it.

Such statements limit, control, and help organize your topic so that you will avoid going off the topic. With this overview of your material, you will find it easier to structure your speech most effectively. Having a statement of the purpose of your speech helps you in all the speech's aspects, from research to delivery. If the subject of your speech requires research, your sense of purpose prevents you from searching out too many sources and therefore becoming entangled in a confusing mass of information. It helps pinpoint what you need to know.

Research Sources

If you plan to do your own research, start with the general reference works found in any public library. Two of the best are *Readers' Guide to Periodical Literature* and *The New York Times Index*. With these you can get a good idea of what has been published in most magazines and in *The New York Times*.

Encyclopedias are good general sources too. If a magazine or newspaper article interests you, check the card catalog in your library to see if the same author has written a book on the subject. Often almanacs are helpful too, especially for statistics. There are many to choose from; among the best are *The World Almanac* and the *Information Please Almanac*. In addition, don't forget that most librarians will be delighted to assist you in your research. They are professionals trained to uncover information. Tell the librarian the purpose of your speech, so he or she will be able to give you specific references.

For business speeches, trade associations are also an excellent source of material. Write to the public-relations director of the trade association you're interested in. The government is a good research source, too. Federal agencies publish a steady stream of pamphlets and brochures on nearly every conceivable subject. Most are free, obtainable by writing to the agency that publishes the material you need. Local government agencies can be helpful also.

Finally, your research may include face-to-face interviews. If you have to speak on a technical subject on which you are relatively uninformed, find out who the experts are. Most experts love to be consulted. If you can't see them, write them a letter requesting sources of information. In most cases, they'll be flattered and will be very helpful.

Organizing Your Material

Organizing simply means putting the materials you want to talk about into their most effective order. Keep in mind the purpose that you have already written down in that single sentence. Then divide that purpose—it's really your central idea—into four or five key thoughts. The experts say that more than five key ideas is too much; the audience won't be able to absorb any more.

These main points cover the important steps, ideas, or questions-and-answers you want to present. They will constitute the main divisions of your speech.

Arrange those points in an order that seems logical and satisfactory to you. One method is through outlining. An outline provides a road map that keeps your speech headed in the direction you want it to go. In skeleton form, an outline may look like this:

I.
    A.
    B.
        1.
        2.
            a.
            b.
                1)
                2)
                    a)
                    b)
                        i
                        ii.
    C.
    D.
II.
    A.
    B.

Such an arrangement helps to clarify and order your thinking. The large Roman numerals represent your main points; other numbers and letters represent the rest of your material, subordinated in a logical way under those major headings. Photocopy Exhibit 13, a checklist to use in assessing your outline, and place it in your "speaking" file.

Creating Your Initial Draft

If you've methodically worked at determining the purpose of your speech, becoming familiar with your material, and outlining it logically, the first draft of your speech should flow easily. Remember: You are writing this speech for *oral* delivery. It should read like a speech, not a technical paper, a memorandum, or a conventional business report. Still, it's always good to be businesslike—that is, simple and direct. Be sure your words sound right to your own trained business ear. Exhibit 14 offers some suggestions for getting your thoughts on paper with maximum effectiveness and minimum struggle.

SHOULD YOU SPEAK FROM THIS DRAFT?

Most experts say no. But writing that first draft imposes a necessary discipline. Most people have a tendency to ramble when talking extemporaneously. It's best to have a firm idea of exactly what you're going to say and how you're going to say it before you speak.

Many beginning speakers feel more comfortable with a written speech. They would do well to bring the written manuscript to the podium and not hesitate to read from it. This is perfectly acceptable on most occasions.

In addition, the program director may ask for a copy of your talk before you deliver it. Usually copies are duplicated

EXHIBIT 13.

Speech outline Checklist

Does my introduction tell the audience in a general way what my speech is about?
Yes_____ No_____

Does the rest of my talk fulfill the promise of the introduction in step-by-step fashion?
Yes_____ No_____

Do I reinforce each assertion with data, anecdote, or illustration?
Yes_____ No_____

Does my speech conclude by reviewing each step briefly and in order?
Yes_____ No_____

How is my ending? Is it memorable? Will I leave them laughing? Worried? Ready to fight?
Yes_____ No_____

---

and given to the press for coverage in newspapers and magazines. You yourself may want to make copies to be distributed to business associates and friends. Major speeches of executives are often printed in pamphlets for wide distribution—to stockholders, employees, or industry leaders.

Preparing a Reading Script

A script consists of your written manuscript designed to be read from the podium. Here are some rules to follow in converting your first draft into a reading script.

EXHIBIT 14.

Suggestions to use in creating a first draft

- "Talk" on paper.

- Use contractions freely.

- Leave out the word "that" whenever possible and avoid "which" like the plague! It is usually used improperly.

- Use direct questions.

- Use personal pronouns.

- It's all right to put prepositions at the end of a sentence.

- Get to the point quickly.

- Write short, snappy sentences; avoid complex ones.

- Use short, punchy words.

- Write for "people" (be human, not stiff).

- Avoid involved sentence structure that starts with such words as "although."

- Choose words for their sound, and avoid words that can be confused with other words (cite/sight).

- Avoid tongue twisters and words a speaker might have trouble pronouncing properly.

- Avoid long strings of adjectives.

- Take time to cover important points; repeat or rephrase your point; listeners can only absorb so much.

- Avoid using too many statistics; keep them as clear and understandable as possible.

- Don't hesitate to quote, but make it clear exactly what you're quoting.

---

1. Have a script typed in very large type.

2. If available, use upper- and lower-case type rather than the all-capital style. With all capitals, it's easy to confuse proper names with ordinary words.

3. For ease of reading, break long paragraphs into shorter ones. To indicate that a thought is continuing, end the earlier paragraph with ellipses (three dots . . .).

4. Never carry sentences or paragraphs over from one page to the next. Let material on a page fall short rather than make the speaker turn the page in the middle of a thought.

5. Indicate pauses with ellipses (. . .) or dashes (—).

6. Commas within sentences aren't easy to see and can be misread as periods. You needn't eliminate them, but it's often better to substitute dashes (—).

7. Never use semicolons or colons; substitute dashes (—).

8. Unless you are absolutely confident as to precisely what words you intend to use, avoid abbreviations and Roman numerals. You can get confused in reading Roman numerals before an audience. For example, *don't* number a sequence of thoughts like this:

   I. Business people need protection from inferior imports.
   II. They also need to improve production.

9. Avoid breaking statistics and certain word combinations at the end of a line.

   Example: In an ordinary working day, we produce $10 million in steel . . .
   You might read this as "ten dollars" and then have to correct yourself.

Example: Here at United Sheet Metal and
Foundry...

Try to keep an entire name or phrase on one line.

10. When the script includes quotations, it is best to insert
the words "quote" and "unquote" (or "end of quote")
to assure that you remember you're quoting.

Example: Recently President Ronald Reagan said—
quote—"We must improve our productivity"—unquote.

11. Underline words for *emphasis*.

12. Effective speakers often repeat words and phrases. It
may look silly in your draft, but don't hesitate to do it
in the script:

Example: We must—must—improve our productivity.

13. Final preparation of the script is the time to insert slang,
mild profanity, or favorite expressions of the speaker
that needn't—and probably shouldn't—appear in the
"official" copy.

Example: The government is always on our necks—
and that's a *hell of a situation*!

Example: Such practices haven't been successful—*it's been like spitting into the wind*!

14. The script is the place for certain personal comments
that you wouldn't want to appear in the official copy.
This refers to comments in the nature of "asides" or "ad
libs."

Example: I'm glad to note that His Honor the Mayor
is here with us tonight—*when I saw him
at the club last night I never thought he'd
make it*!

> Example: Our Medford plant is doing extremely well—*I drove by on the way to this meeting and the superintendent, Charlie Johnson—most of you know Charlie— he asked me to tell you that he's got everything under control.*

15. Rehearse your speech out loud. If changes are needed, make them. That's also a good time to *time* the length of the speech.

Speechwriting in Action

Veteran public speaker Ben Brodinsky sums up his approach to the speechwriting process:

> My written first draft is often no more than a series of notes, which I jot down rather rapidly. Then I work on those notes, often rearranging them and putting in new ideas and better phrases.
>
> My next step is to talk the speech into a tape recorder. That way I know how much time it takes, and where I need to strengthen and where to cut. Finally I prepare a polished draft, which I duplicate and use for publication purposes, if such opportunities arise.
>
> But I almost never use a script when I actually deliver the talk. It's there to fall back on if I need it, but I try to give all my speeches extemporaneously. I think they sound better and are more convincing that way. But, of course, I put just as much preparation and writing into them as I would into any other kind of writing.

DELIVERING
THE SPEECH

You're well prepared. Now the moment of truth is at hand. Don't panic! Approach the podium with a confident air, acknowledge your introduction, and take all the time you need to get started.

"I've seen speakers plunge into their material, rattled by the suspicion that the microphone isn't working properly," says speech consultant Lee Bowman. "If you have any doubts, stop. Ask whether they can hear you in the last row. If your throat gets dry, stop again; take a sip of water. You'll put your audience and yourself at ease. In fact, you'll come through as a real pro."

A couple of easy quips may help break any tension. For instance, if you have to raise or lower the microphone, you might say, "I have to adjust this for inflation." Or, "Any of you who can hear me may want to change seats with someone who can't." The audience reponse to such banter can reinforce your confidence so that you get off to a good start. When you're confident, you'll act naturally, without stiffness or "airs," and this will contribute to the effectiveness of what you say.

PHYSICAL ADJUSTMENTS

To gain physical poise, avoid shifting your weight from foot to foot or swaying from side to side. Don't rock back and forth. Be aware that how you stand in front of an audience affects its perception of you. Assume a posture of "relaxed alertness," said Bert E. Bradley, professor of Speech and Communications at Auburn University. "Don't worry about what to do with your hands. Just be natural. Remember that those appendages at the ends of your arms do not look as big and awkward to the listeners as you think they do."

Bradley recommends movement, not only to dispel nervousness but to improve your presentation. For instance, movement can be used to emphasize a transition from one point to another. At the conclusion of a point, you may pause and then move to another position on the platform before beginning the next point. This movement serves as a figurative bridge between the two points and emphasizes to the listeners that you have moved to a new idea.

One of the most effective ways to reveal your deep-seated feeling is through your facial expressions. When you look at your audience with an alert, expressive face and an occasional smile you tell them nonverbally that you are happy to be there talking to them.

Appropriate gestures also help. But be sure they look natural, not awkward or staged. "When you do gesture," according to the Bethlehem Steel manual, "make it decisive and not halfhearted. If you point, point boldly!"

Exhibit 15 offers some tips for physical-relaxation exercises prior to your speechmaking.

EXHIBIT 15.

Relaxation tips

Here are some suggestions for physical relaxation to prepare yourself to give your best speaking effort.

1. Stand erect, like a private in the army. Support weight evenly on both feet. Tense all the muscles in your legs, throw your shoulders back, open your eyes like you just saw a ghost.

2. Relax. Pretend you got the at-ease command. Slowly revolve your head, letting the rest of your body sort of hang. Imagine all your muscles as tissues drifting lightly to the ground.

3. Keep working the muscles of your neck, revolving your head left and right. Let your head fall forward, then stretch it back.

4. Hunch your shoulders and inhale. Bring them down and exhale. Circle them in opposite directions, like a football player adjusting his shoulder pads.

5. Grasp your hands behind your back, then turn them palms out. Stretch your arms up and down and move your torso sideways.

6. Let your jaw fall open. Inhale deeply until a yawn is induced.

    Now you're ready to go.

If something bothers you, take care of it. If you itch, scratch. If your throat gets dry, take a sip of water. Audiences admire an imperturbable person.

Don't panic if catastrophe strikes. But don't plunge ahead blindly as though nothing happened. If a waiter drops a load of dishes, or there's an explosion across the hall, don't ignore it. Say something about it. Otherwise, the audience will think you're oblivious to reality.

If any disturbance distracts your listeners, wait for it to subside or make an appropriate remark, such as, "Well, in my business we're used to competition."

UTILIZING PROPS

Handling props effectively helps your audience grasp your ideas more quickly—seeing is believing. What's more, props add a touch of showmanship.

Ben Brodinsky uses a chalkboard to create suspense and hold his audience's attention. After he is introduced, Brodinsky simply nods in acknowledgment and then, without a word to the audience, takes a certain amount of time to draw a ladder on the chalkboard with rungs labeled "P," "C," and "D." Then Brodinsky returns to the podium and begins to talk. He talks for fifteen or twenty minutes, never referring to, or even looking at, the chalkboard. Needless to say, the audience is puzzled and its curiosity grows. Finally, at a preselected point in the talk, Brodinsky turns to the chalkboard and explains the ladder and the letters— a key part of his message carefully presented to achieve maximum dramatic effect.

Mark Hammer, formerly a marketing specialist at the Bristol Myers Company, developed the following suggestions to help you use props to best advantage.

Chalkboard

- Print, if your handwriting isn't perfect.

- Use large letters. Remember the people in back!

- Know what you're going to write before you start.

- Stand sidewise while you write.

- Talk as you write.

- Use colored chalk, different colors for different points. Underscore, circle, and use arrows for emphasis.

Prepared chart pages

- When you reveal a chart page, always read all the copy aloud before expanding on any one point.

- Practice turning the chart pages until you can do it smoothly and easily.

- Make light pencil notes on charts for a smooth transition from one point to another.

- On new chart pads, bend up one corner of each page so that it can be turned easily.

- Gesture toward the charts to focus audience attention.

Posters

- Be sure they are in the proper sequence and placed high enough for good visibility.

- Conceal posters until you are ready to reveal them (face inward on an easel or cover with paper or cloth).

- Practice handling them until it goes smoothly.

Printed materials

- Be thoroughly familiar with them and give them the emphasis they deserve.

- Guide your audience through a brief review of each handout after you have given it to them.

Sound slide film and 16mm movie projectors

- Set the projector on a solid table far enough and high enough from the screen so that the picture fills the screen and no heads block the view.

- Use a remote speaker placed at the front of room. Cover the speaker cable with tape.

- Check the electrical outlets to be sure current is correct for equipment. Cover or tape all cords and cables if people will be walking over them.

- Make certain you can darken the room as required by your film.

- Clean projector lens and film gate.

- Thread film beforehand, check focus, and adjust tone and volume controls for the size of room.

- For the slidefilm projector, use the focus frame, then advance to the title frame.

- Always have an extra projection lamp and exciter lamp (for 16mm sound) available and know how to insert them.

Slide projectors

- Be sure slides are in the correct sequence.

- Ensure they are inserted properly for correct image on screen.

- Use automatic tray load whenever possible.

- For paper mounted slides, ensure an adequate blower system to avoid heat damage to slides.

Overhead projectors

- Place projector on a solid table, far enough away to fill screen. Use comfortable working height, without blocking the audience's view of the screen.

- The beam from the projector should be at right angles to the plane of the screen.

- Place the projection slides on the machine so you can read the copy (unless you are using rear projection).

- Keep projection slides flat.

- Practice changing the slides so that screen is never blank.

- Practice any lift-offs, drop-ons, or other special effects that may be included on the slides.

- Achieve "progressive disclosure" of a list of points by sliding a sheet of cardboard down the slide.

- Use a pointer or a pencil to point out items on the slide, casting a similar shadow on the screen.

- Use a grease pencil to mark or write on the surface of the slide so the mark or writing will appear on the screen.

Opaque projector

- Use for printed material and photographs.

- Create a totally darkened room.

- Mount loose sheets on light cardboard to prevent "curling" during projection.

- Focus on the largest unit to be projected to ensure all of it will be on screen. (Smaller units will not fill screen, so pre-check to make sure the group will be able to see necessary printing and photographic details.)

Recordings

- Set up recording equipment beforehand.

- Have record in place on turntable.

- Check for correct turntable speed for the record.

- Set volume knobs so that sound level is correct.

- Adjust tone control for best voice quality.

- Practice starting the recording for smooth, fast operation.

Tape recorders

- Set tape recorder for correct playing speed. (Usually 7½ inches per second, but check label on tape.)

- Thread tape correctly before meeting and test run. (Dull side of tape should be against magnetic sound head.)

- Plug in external speaker for best tone quality.

- Mark volume and tone levels with a grease pencil.

- Cue tape up so leader is almost past playing head.

- Be sure you are familiar with all controls.

- Always allow time for tape recorder to warm up.

- Rewind tape after each use.

Screens

- Front projection screens may be beaded, matte finish, or lenticular. The lenticular screen permits a wider angle of viewing than the other two types.

- Rear projection screens are usually matte finish.

- Place screen high enough so that everyone has an unobstructed view. The bottom edge of the screen should be about 4½ feet off the floor. Do not place screen too high or viewing will be uncomfortable.

- In an oblong room, place the screen parallel to the shorter dimension.

- Keystoning is the distorted enlargement of the screen image at the top of the picture. To avoid keystoning, the plane of the screen should be at a right angle to the center line of projection.

- If you cannot raise the projector high enough to avoid keystoning, tilt the screen to achieve the correct angle relationship.

Audience placement

- Here are rules-of-thumb for seating your audience in relation to the position of the screen:

1. Closest viewer—no less than two screen widths' distance.

2. Farthest viewer—no more than six screen widths' distance.

3. Widest angles of viewing for maximum light intensity on screen:

   a. beaded screen, 22 degrees from center line of projection

   b. matte finish screen, 30 degrees from center line of projection

   c. lenticular screen, 50 degrees from center line of projection

INJECTING HUMOR

Humor generally adds to a speech, but it is certainly not obligatory for all speeches. As a matter of fact, it can be disastrously inappropriate on certain occasions. Also, you may not feel comfortable with jokes. In that case, don't feel that you have to put them into your talk just because they're expected. Better to be known for seriousness of purpose than for inept humor.

On the other hand, humor persuades an audience to your point of view in ways that almost nothing else can. It can bring bounce and grace and good feeling to your speech. Never underestimate the value—and sheer joy—of hearing an audience roar with appreciation of your jokes or, better still, your wit.

Bob Orben, a professional humorist who conducts humor workshops for corporate speakers and communicators, stresses relevance in the selection of humor. "Is the line or story applicable to your business, your area of expertise, or occasions and events you may possibly be concerned with?" he asks. "For example, do you have some good retirement and leisure time material to call on if you speak at a retirement dinner?"

Orben advocates collecting quips, jokes, and anecdotes on 3-by 5-inch file cards according to potential use and subject matter. "Cross-index liberally," he says. "If you have a joke about getting a cake for your birthday that could be used as a speech opener, make up four identical cards and file them under openers, birthdays, gifts, and food. As the file grows, you may miss a joke that is ideal for a specific speech unless it is filed under the subject and category you are researching."

Guidelines for Humor

1. Responses to introductions should be modest; make gentle fun of yourself; at all costs, avoid seeming pompous and self-important.

2. Don't offend; ethnic jokes are always in poor taste. But witty humor poking gentle fun at certain groups—accountants, or lawyers, or politicians—is acceptable.

3. Never, never allow yourself to get flustered if a joke falls flat.

4. Good storytellers don't telegraph their material. Don't say, "Here's a funny story for you . . ."

5. Always avoid long and possibly tedious jokes. If one doesn't click, the speaker is in bad shape. Except in rare cases, keep them short.

6. Whenever possible and appropriate, tie in humor with personalities at the event. A simple example would be,

"Your president was telling me about the insurance business all through dinner, and that reminds me..." Or, "I remember a fellow who used to work for me—a big, husky guy with a loud voice—like your chairman..." Or refer to a friend in the audience.

7. When you want to use a joke from, for instance, a magazine, don't pick up exact words. Study it. Consider how it will sound—not how well it reads. Adapt it for the spoken word.

8. Humor is almost invariably best when you tie it into something of current and immediate interest, such as today's financial news, or a headline in the morning paper, or something that occurred in the course of the program.

9. Always keep the occasion and the group clearly in mind in planning the humor you intend to use. Was there a golf tournament for the group that afternoon? Use golf jokes. What is the significance of the date? Is it a commemorative date? Did some special occasion occur just before the event, or will one soon be forthcoming? Such facts can provide inspiration for uncovering the right material.

There are many books of jokes, anecdotes, and quips for speechmakers. Back issues of such magazines as *Reader's Digest* are helpful.

SEEK OBJECTIVE RATINGS

You can get valuable assistance from objective observers that will go a long way toward helping you become a more effective speaker. Simply ask them to fill out copies of the speech analysis rating scale in Exhibit 16.

EXHIBIT 16.

A speech rating scale for observers' analysis

Name_____

Topic_____

ITEMS	COMMENTS	Rating
SUBJECT: Of interest, significance? Adapted to speaker, audience, occasion? Subject properly narrowed?		
ANALYSIS: Approach to subject original, interesting? Central idea, goal, purpose clear? Logical division into significant, interesting, subordinate ideas?		
MATERIAL: Specific, valid, relevant, sufficient, interesting? Properly distributed throughout speech? Adapted to audience?		

ITEMS	COMMENTS	R a t i n g
ORGANIZATION: Introduction, body, conclusion? Clear arrangement of ideas? Pattern of development adapted to ideas and audience?		
LANGUAGE: Clear, accurate, varied, vivid? Correct, appropriate standard usage? In conversational mode?		
ADJUSTMENT OF SPEAKER: Poised, at ease, communicative, direct? Personality pleasing, projected to audience? Aware of audience reaction to the speech?		

ITEMS	COMMENTS	Rating
BODILY ACTION: Is speaker animated? Is posture, action constructive or distracting? Adapted to ideas and occasion?		
VOICE: Pleasing, adequate, distracting? Varied or monotonous in pitch, intensity, quality? Expressive of logical and emotional meanings?		
ARTICULATION AND PRONUNCIATION: Articulation clear, correct, slurred, muffled? Defective sounds? Acceptable standard of pronunciation?		
FLUENCY: Extemporaneous, conversational? Varied, monotonous, too fast, too slow? Adapted to ideas, speaking situation?		

ITEMS	COMMENTS	Rating
GENERAL EFFEC-TIVENESS: Listeners attentive, interested? Speaker's goal maintained, achieved in speech?		
RATING SCALE:		Total

1. poor
2. inadequate
3. fair
4. average

5. good
6. excellent
7 superior

OBSERVER

The frank criticism of people who hear you can help immeasurably in identifying the flaws in your performance that might otherwise go undetected. All speech professionals recommend that you need structured criticism of your performance in order to achieve maximum effectiveness. If a colleague or subordinate is scheduled to make a speech, copy Exhibit 16 and conduct your own analysis of the speech for him or her.

12

ESTABLISHING
YOUR CREDIBILITY

Assume that you've done your background work and you're happy with the draft of your speech. Now is a good time to ask questions: Will the audience accept these claims I've made? Will they have full confidence that I am telling the truth?

"Selling" a product, a program, an idea, or even a point of view is not as easy these days as it used to be. Today's speakers face new problems in the form of increasingly skeptical audiences. To their dismay, even veteran speech-makers have found some of their favorite messages being greeted with sighs and bored glances, an outbreak of throat clearing, or—and nothing could be worse—mocking laughter.

Be prepared for the change in public attitudes: Audiences are not as submissive to authority as they used to be. Numerous surveys and polls have documented a worldwide decline in cofidence in institutions, especially business. For the modern public speaker, it's a challenge to overcome.

How? The first step is to give your own credibility serious attention and take conscious measures to reinforce it.

"Fortunately, much can be done to make your presentation believable," said William L. Hennefrund, a professional speech writer who counsels business people in such organizations as UniRoyal and the American Stock Exchange. Hennefrund offers eight important points to consider in dealing with the problem of credibility.

EIGHT STEPS TO CREDIBILITY

1. *Be honest with your audience.* "Honesty" can be difficult. Naturally, if you care about your credibility, you'll be open and direct in the presentation of facts. But it's dangerously easy to overdramatize or to "liven up" material to the point where "truth" gets distorted. In your eagerness to present your case, be careful not to exaggerate or quote statements or figures out of context.

   Philip Lesley, a veteran public-relations counselor and an experienced speaker himself, put it this way: "A speaker shouldn't try to mislead an audience by slanting his material. The first time your audience suspects that you're trying to mislead them, the speech is lost."

   Even sentence structure can pose a trap to your credibility. Make your points directly. If statements are hidden underneath involved phrasing or excessive rhetoric, an audience will sense some deception, even if they don't know exactly what it is you are, or are not, saying.

   For example: "In terms of the conclusions drawn from the analysis of prior pay periods among individuals who were accustomed to biweekly pay periods, no appreciable benefit to employees or to the department was determined in the event of installation of a program to increase the frequency of pay periods, regardless of opposing suggestions."

Note the buried message: "Employees requested weekly pay periods, we decided to keep the biweekly system." Surely, the audience is going to suspect that something has been overlooked or ignored. Once the listener has untangled the syllables, he will want to know the extent of the study and the reasons for the decision. A point that needs such overblown language for explanation or cover-up should be discarded altogether.

2. *Know both sides of the argument.* You may not have to deal with opposition arguments in the course of your presentation, but just knowing them will endow your statements with more conviction.

A securities industry speaker who gives fifteen to twenty speeches a year on investment said:

> I try to get across the point that a good investment climate is good for the country. But a lot of people in my audience think investing is just another form of gambling. At first, that seemed unbelievable to me. But I figured I'd better get to know all I could about that point of view. That effort paid off. If anyone raises the point, I probably know more about gambling than they do. Now I can convincingly make the distinction.

3. *Make sure your audience knows you're the expert.* It isn't enough just to know your subject. You must establish your expertise with the audience immediately.

Sometimes the program chairman reads a brief biography of the speaker. But just as often, the speaker has to offer his or her own credentials. You can do it by using specific and graphic phrases: "In some twenty years of counseling unemployed people..." or "Four years of study of this question convinced me that...."

When facing a skeptical audience you may want to emphasize your all-around expertise on the matter in question. Government or business representatives use this to their advantage by saying: "I've been in both business and government—I've seen this problem from both sides. And I've concluded...." Or you can claim: "I've discussed and debated this issue many times with [name of someone who takes the opposite view], and while I respect his feelings...."

The point is, convey to the audience that you understand all points of view, particularly the opposition's.

4. *Raise questions yourself.* A powerful boost to your credibility is achieved if you raise "opposition" questions yourself—particularly if the audience is aware of criticisms that have been made of your position. "When you raise questions yourself, it shows you are fairminded," said a New York banker who regularly faces groups of disenchanted stockholders. "It establishes that you are open-minded to criticisms and have thought them out."

A word of caution: Having raised the question, do not flatly contradict it. This is particularly important when speaking to a general audience with diverse interests and attitudes. Casting an argument in terms of good versus bad is customary on television when a subject must be covered in thirty seconds. In public speaking, more time and background are involved. Raise the opposition question, concede that it seems to have some validity, then give the arguments that outweigh it.

5. *Prove it with facts.* Statistics can improve your case, but be careful how you use them. Too many can be boring.

Faced with a need to use many statistics, some speakers try to avoid the problem by simplifying: "We just about doubled productivity." That approach by itself, however, blurs the subject. You gain credibility if you use exact figures, and there are a number of ways to do that. For example: "We just about doubled productivity—from 150 units per man-hour to 294 units, 96 percent to be exact—and I think that proves...." Another way is to use the rounded, simplified figure in the speech, then make available the exact figures in printed form.

6. *Create your own survey.* Speakers often quote surveys and studies to support a point. Another device: Make your own survey. If the validity of your survey methods is clear, your point will be made convincingly, and your talk will generate more audience interest. You will have contributed something new to the area of concern, something your audience has never heard before.

You don't have to question a great number of people; about twenty is usually enough. Just don't give the impression that your survey was nationwide. Depending on the nature of your question, you may have queried business associates, neighbors, customers, or total strangers. Your audience is going to listen when you say: "I wondered about [the subject] myself. So I decided to ask several small-company business people what they thought. And I think their answers will surprise you as much as they surprised me."

7. *Cite authorities that are accepted by your audience.* Check quotations in your speech to make sure you've

used the most credible authorities. Your arguments will gain greater acceptance if they are supported by authorities whose opinions are respected by your particular audience. A college or university audience is likely to be fairly sophisticated about the views of well-known professors and may have strong reactions to their opinions. For most audiences, citing a university "authority" will almost always lend credence. The observations of bankers, economists, journalists, conservationists, and consumer activists can also create a feeling of professionalism in your speech.

8. *Invite questions from the audience.* Speakers with a point of view welcome the chance to answer questions from the audience; they regard it as another opportunity to gain credibility. But it's not easy to answer questions from an audience, especially from a skeptical one. To plan an effective response, an experienced speaker tries to anticipate every question that might be asked. This effort may take as much time and care as preparing the speech itself. A speaker who is really prepared will even have back-up data to cite for a few of those responses.

What if you don't know the answer? Say so. Then go quickly to the next question. What if the question requires a long, complicated answer? Answer briefly. Then ask how many in the audience are interested in the matter and offer to discuss it further with those people afterward. If a question is hostile, be sure not to show annoyance. After all, you invited the questions.

Above all, don't turn an "easy" question into a repeat of your speech or the delivery of a new one. Keep your answers short. That will enable you to answer as many questions as you wish—and will make the people in your audience feel that they are a part of your presentation.

When people become active participants in your "program"—not merely targets for your opinions—it's time to congratulate yourself. They may or may not agree with you, but they will give you high marks for integrity. And that, in these days of skeptical audiences, is no small achievement.

THE
ACTION-ORIENTED
SPEECH

The late Dale Carnegie, world-renowned orator and teacher of public speaking, developed what he called the "Magic Formula" for speech construction. Simply put, Carnegie's formula was this: Start your talk by giving the details of a dramatic or otherwise attention-getting example, an anecdote or incident that graphically illustrates the main idea you want to get across. In specific, clear-cut terms give the point of your talk and tell exactly what you want the audience to do. Then give the reason why your listeners should do what you tell them—that is, highlight the advantage or benefit to be gained by the listener when he or she does what you ask.

This highly successful formula works because it gains attention and focuses quickly on the main point of your message. It avoids such boring introductory remarks as "I didn't have time to prepare this talk very well" or "When your chairman asked me to speak on this subject, I wondered why he selected me."

THE MAGIC FORMULA
AT WORK

"Audiences are not interested in apologies or excuses," Carnegie said. "They want action. With the magic formula, you give them action from the opening word."

This formula is especially well suited for short talks, because it is based upon a certain amount of suspense. Listeners become interested in the story you are telling, but they are not aware of the point you're trying to make until you've completed the opening story or anecdote.

"In cases where demands are made upon the audience," Carnegie said, "this is almost a prerequisite for success. No speaker who wants his listeners to dig deep in their pockets for a cause or a product will get very far by starting to say 'Ladies and Gentlemen, I'm here to collect $25 from each of you.' Instead you'd see a scramble for the exits!"

Carnegie's magic formula suggests that the speaker, instead of merely asking for donations, describe a visit to a children's hospital where he or she saw a particularly poignant case of need, a little child who lacked financial help for an operation in a distant hospital. Then ask for contributions. Approaching the appeal in this way improves the speaker's chances of getting support, according to Carnegie.

Here's an example of this kind of action-getting appeal, used by noted industrialist Leland Stowe to generate support of the United Nations' Appeal for Children:

> I pray that I'll never have to do it again. Can there be anything much worse than to put only a peanut between a child and death? I hope you'll never have to do it, and live with the memory of it afterward. If you had heard their voices and

seen their eyes, on that January day in the bomb-scarred workers' district of Athens... Yet all I had left was a half-pound can of peanuts. As I struggled to open it, dozens of ragged kids held me in a vise of frantically clawing bodies. Scores of mothers, with babes in their arms, pushed and fought to get within arm's reach. They held their babies out toward me. Tiny hands of skin and bone stretched convulsively. I tried to make every peanut count.

In their frenzy they nearly swept me off my feet. Nothing but hundreds of hands: begging hands, clutching hands, despairing hands; all of them pitifully little hands. One salted peanut here, and one peanut there. Six peanuts knocked from my fingers, and a savage scramble of emaciated bodies at my feet. Another peanut here, and another peanut there. Hundreds of hands, reaching and pleading, hundreds of eyes with the light of hope flickering out. I stood there helpless, an empty blue can in my hand... Yes, I hope it will never happen to you.

Carnegie's magic formula, based on the narrative of an incident or story, is often used in advertising with great success. American Express sells its credit-card service by asking magazine readers to tell their personal stories of how their American Express credit card helped them out of financial dilemmas or how the company's service came to their aid in difficult situations. The company reprints the best stories, with graphic details, and then goes on to the point of the ad: "Subscribe to American Express Credit Card Service, and you may be helped in a similar way."

Eveready Batteries has used the same formula for years. In a series of print, radio, and television ads, stories explain how beams from flashlights, equipped with Eveready Batteries, saved victims of accidents, storms, and other disasters.

YOUR OWN MAGIC FORMULA

"A single personal experience that taught you a lesson you will never forget is the first requisite of the persuasive action talk," Carnegie said. "With this kind of incident you can impel audiences to act. If it happened to you, your listeners reason, it can happen to them. And they'd better take your advice by doing what you ask them to do."

Here are some capsule suggestions for putting the formula to work in your action speeches.

• Fill your example with relevant detail—use concrete, colorful language that will re-create the incident so that the audience relives it with you. Paint word pictures. Example: The road went suddenly uphill and into a blackness of woods. As the speeding Volvo reached the top I saw, too late, that the northern slope of the hill, still untouched by the sun's rays, was like a river of ice. I had a fleeting glimpse of the two wildly careering cars in front of us and then we went into a skid. . . .

• Relive your experience as you relate it—the more action and excitement you can put into the retelling of your incident, the greater the impression on your audience.

• State your point—tell exactly what you want the audience to do. Relating the incident may consume most of the time of your talk—especially if it's short. So you now must make a forthright, direct assertion. Make the point brief and specific. Make it easy for your listeners to act upon. State it with force and conviction.

• Give the reason or benefit the audience may expect—keep it simple. Give only one or two reasons. Don't confuse your audience by listing a number of benefits.

Concentrate on the single reason that you think will most strongly motivate your audience.

ORGANIZING THE ACTION SPEECH

Clark S. Carlile, professor of speech, emeritus, at Idaho State University, worked out the preparation of action speeches in step-by-step fashion. First, decide exactly what action you will ask your audience to take. This must be definite. It must not be a generalized or hazy idea about some vague action. Until you know absolutely and positively the specific action you want, you are not ready to begin preparing your speech. A complete-sentence statement of your specific purpose is required. Write it out so that you can have it in front of you throughout your entire preparation.

Having decided on the specific action you want from your audience, organize your speech as follows:

1. Tell generally and in some detail what is currently happening in regard to the subject you are talking about. Give facts, examples, illustrations, and testimony to make your ideas clear but do not spend too much time on this part of your speech.

2. Show how this is affecting the lives of your listeners. Explain how it is costing them money, damaging their community, retarding their personal advancement, endangering their lives or their children's lives, giving them a bad name; that it is unsanitary, detrimental to community progress, and so on. Use whatever appeals are necessary to make your listeners see that they are

affected personally. Be sure to give evidence to support these appeals. Make this point clear but do not overwork it.

3. Show what can be done to correct or change the situation and indicate the action necessary for your audience to take. The action you suggest at this time, along with your arguments to show that it should be taken, will make up the major portion of your speech.

4. Concerning that action:

    •   Show how your audience will benefit personally and/ or as a group if the action you suggest is taken. Be specific in pointing out what the audience stands to gain from the action.

    •   Appeal to the desire for money and health, security, fame, social status, prestige, or recognition.

    •   Show how easy it is to take the action.

    •   Show how the audience can afford it if it involves money or goods.

    •   Show that the time can be spared if that's what it involves.

    •   Tell the audience specifically when to do it. Give the date and the time.

    •   Tell the audience where to do it. Name the exact location and supply directions about how to get there.

    •   Identify the equipment that will be needed (if any).

    •   Give the names and addresses of specific persons to be contacted and when to make the contacts—the hours those persons are available.

- If a petition is to be signed, have available several copies and writing instruments to be circulated.

- Tell how to perform the action if there is any question about it.

5. Reiterate briefly the "negative things" that could happen if the action you suggest is not taken. Contrast this by briefly repeating the "positive things" that will follow if the audience does follow your suggestions. Conclude with well-planned remarks stating your confidence that they will do the right thing.

TIPS ON GIVING THE ACTION SPEECH

1. Say "we" when speaking to your audience. If you constantly refer to your listeners as "you," they may wonder what you yourself are going to do about the action you are asking them to take. If you say "we," the audience immediately includes you as one of them.

2. Take every opportunity to use appropriate props—drawings, pictures, diagrams, graphs. Demonstrate a product, if at all feasible. If you have a movie on the subject, be sure to show it. Any group involvement can be used to help get your audience in a receptive mood.

THE
INFORMATIONAL
SPEECH

Most speeches made by business people involve technical, financial, or political subjects. The primary aim is not to motivate but simply to explain and inform. Here are some explain-and-inform situations you are likely to face as you work your way into the upper echelons of the corporate hierarchy:

1. a proposed budget to division and department heads at your company's annual review conference

2. the preliminary design of a new plant to the executive committee

3. your company's progress for the past year at the annual stockholders' meeting

4. your company's strengths, new products, and future prospects to security analysts

5. description of a new method of making a product to assembly-line workers

6. a talk to a community group about your company's plans to expand locally and what impact you expect that action will have on the employment situation

Such speeches are not quite as simple as they may sound. Rarely is it wise to "talk off the top of your head" in such situations. You will lose your audience quickly if you ramble, if your words aren't precise, if you get lost in a welter of statistics or complicated explanations.

You will succeed only if you present accurate information in such a way that the audience will listen to, understand, and remember it. Assuming that you have analyzed the context of your talk and its audience and have chosen a clear purpose, your energies then turn to matters of support, structure, and style.

DIFFERENT APPROACHES
FOR DIFFERENT AUDIENCES

Give examples to illustrate a point whenever appropriate. Make these examples relate to the audience. In explaining a new, "state-of-the-art" computer introduced by the Digital Equipment Company, President Ken Olsen described this model as the first to "engage in a really fantastic playing of the word-game Scrabble." That speech was to stockholders, a mixed group with varied interests and education. In front of security analysts, Olsen didn't mention Scrabble. Instead, he stressed the new computer's applications in the telephone industry, a promising market. In another speech on the same subject to engineers, Olsen mentioned neither Scrabble nor the telephone market. He concentrated instead on the technical developments that made the new computer possible. Same subject, but different approaches for different audiences. That's the major component of effective speeches that explain and inform.

This can be done even when facing a diverse audience that has little or no prior knowledge of the subject. Speaking to such an audience, Major General John C. Toomay of the United States Air Force Systems Command used two familiar examples to support his point that "the field of transportation has profited from our work in space":

> As you board a commercial jet aircraft to take a business trip . . . you may be comforted to know that the guidance system is a direct descendant of one of this country's major space efforts. The guidance system is called a 'carousal' and was developed for the Apollo program . . . .
>
> The automobile tire has been improved by knowledge gained from outer space experience too. From research for the Apollo program a tire was developed that would maintain its flexibility under extreme temperature changes. This technology, which increases traction and eliminates the need for studs, has been incorporated into winter radial tires.

Note that Toomay used examples that were relevant to both the subject and his audience.

Utilizing Visual Aids

Graphics and visual aids can be of great help in supporting your information speeches. Vernon Plotkin, while an audio/visual specialist at the Raytheon Company of Lexington, Massachusetts, claimed that good visual aids have four main characteristics: clarity, adequate size, accuracy, and attractiveness.

Clarity. Avoid complex and highly detailed visual aids. Try for a large format with a minimum of detail. When explaining complex subjects, break down the subject into a series of simple steps on a chalkboard or an overhead projector.

Adequate size.   Be sure that all your visual aids can be seen by everyone in the audience. Check it out beforehand by setting up your visual aid and then sitting in the seat farthest from the platform.

Accuracy.   Graphs, diagrams, drawings, and maps have a way of getting distorted from conception to execution. Go over them for accuracy and precision before you speak.

Attractiveness.   Sloppy visuals indicate sloppy research to most audiences. That's a death knell to your credibility! Besides, well-designed, crisply executed visuals enhance your performance immeasurably. Consider all the factors: creativity, neatness, color selection, balance, and proportion.

"Use your visual aids to help prove specific points," Plotkin advised. "The speaker's words should be carefully coordinated and integrated with what the audience is seeing. A visual aid left standing there doesn't help a speech; it detracts from it."

Plan where to fit each visual aid into the speech, prepare a transition to introduce it to the audience, describe its essential elements, make your point, and then move smoothly into the remainder of your speech. Here's how to do it:

Transition   "The graph to my right illustrates our sales
to aid: figures for first quarter 1983.

Description of key elements:	"Note that the vertical axis depicts the rate of sales. The horizontal axis identifies the weeks from January 1.
Main point:	"You can see that January was a slow month—that's more or less expected—but as we move into February things began to pick up. In March we took off like a rocket!
Transition to next point:	"Now, what's the outlook for the rest of the year? Based on our performance so far . . ."

AVOID BORING YOUR AUDIENCE

The specter that haunts every informational speaker is the danger that he may turn out to be—*boring*! It's a healthy fear. If your audience is bored, you can't possibly accomplish the purpose of your speech.

To avoid boring your audience, strive for the qualities enumerated by Chester Davis, a marketing specialist based in Waltham, Massachusetts:

1. Use all the attention-getting devices appropriate to the audience and the occasion

2. Be brief

3. Be clear

Attention-Getting Devices

All audio/visual aids fall in this category. So does the language you use, the figures of speech you employ, the parallels, examples, and comparisons with which you make your points.

According to Davis, language properly used can hold attention in nearly all situations: "Inspirational flourishes and poetic metaphors may be out of place but that doesn't mean speakers have to be humdrum and monotonous in their use of language. Use questions to break up the monotony. Try a few figures of speech and, by all means, quote prominent authorities when you can."

Another suggestion is to mention plainly as you go along that you are taking up first one point and then another: "My first point is this: . . ." You can be as blunt as that. When you've discussed the first point, go on to the second.

Example: You have been selected by the national trade association to give an important talk to the leaders of your industry. "I have chosen to speak tonight on the subject 'The Challenge of Inflation' for two reasons. In the first place . . ." After you've given your primary reason, you continue: "In the second place . . ." You keep up this orderly enumeration throughout your talk, making it clear to your listeners how you are leading them, point by point, to your conclusion.

Be Brief

Determine the point you want to make, tailor your material to build to a conclusion, and do not allow digressions and irrelevancies to creep in.

But, as speech specialists emphasize, even a speech containing only relevant facts can vary greatly in length, depending on language choices. Former U.S. President Woodrow Wilson made famous this complaint: "I would have made this speech shorter if I had time." Pruning needless words requires much time in preparation, but it pays big dividends when you make the speech. It not only saves time but simultaneously increases the impact of your message.

The following examples show how you can trim words by using the active voice, fewer prepositional phrases, and fewer adjectives.

Wordy: "It is my opinion that our advertising budget ought to be increased." (12 words)

Short: "We should increase our advertising budget." (6 words)

Wordy: "It was last year that plans were formulated by our shipping department for an expansion of the Night and Day Service." (21 words)

Short: "Last year our shipping department planned to expand the Night and Day Service." (13 words)

Wordy: "The subject of injuries to employees is a most important matter and therefore ought to be considered immediately." (18 words)

Short: "Employee injuries demand our immediate attention." (6 words)

Be Clear

Davis offers five ways to clarify ideas: negative definition, positive definition, restatement, comparison, and specificity.

Negative definition.   Negative definitions can help clear up misconceptions that an audience may have about a word or concept. In a speech to the Small Business Association of New England, Brooks Fenno, a Boston-based marketing consultant, used the technique of negative definition when delivering an informative talk about marketing practices: "Marketing is not a trick or a gimmick or a set of ploys. It's not a get-rich-quick scheme, a shill, a plot to fool the public into buying things it doesn't want or need. It's not solely advertising or salesmanship or distribution...."

Positive definition.   Fenno then proceeded to give a positive definition of marketing: "Marketing, to put it briefly, is a view of the entire business process as an integrated effort to identify the customers and their needs and to mold, promote, and distribute a product or service to fill those needs."

Restatement.   Often it helps to repeat an idea in different words, both for emphasis and clarity. Dr. Karl Menninger, founder of the Menninger Clinic for Psychiatric Research, used restatement in addressing a lay audience: "The fourth observation...is that some patients may have a mental illness and then get well, and then may even get 'weller.' I mean they get better than they were before."

Comparison.   A speaker can give listeners a point of reference by relating an idea to something with which the audience can easily identify. John E. Murray did that in a speech as vice president of the American Association of Railroads: "I am not saying that there are no bad lawyers. What I say is that the popular, blanket denunciation of lawyers is bad. You might as well denounce the sun for giving you a burn, rather than praise it as a source of life."

Specificity.   An uneasiness arises when information lacks concrete detail. Consider this real-life description of a company's plans to build a new plant by a vice president of a manufacturing company to a gathering of local residents: "Well, the idea is to put the building—it will be a large building with quite a few employees—just off the Northfield Road but close enough to town to give our trucks access to the state highway. I know you're concerned about the dumping of toxic chemicals, but I'm here to assure you that we've discussed this matter with anti-pollution authorities, and we're putting into effect an excellent system. . . ."

Such a description leaves so many unanswered questions—exactly how big is the building? How many employees is "quite a few"? What is that "excellent system" comprised of? The audience is almost certain to go away with deep suspicions about the desirability of permitting that company in the town. In a situation such as this, the more detail the better. No fear of boring an audience when vital interests are on the line.

By contrast, here is an excerpt from a speech by Charles Schalliol, an expert on air pollution, describing a thick fog that hit Donora, Pennsylvania, and held fumes from the big steel mills at ground level: "Before the clouds of fog lifted from Donora, twenty had died, and 6,000, or half the population, were bedridden. Donora was the site of America's first major air pollution disaster.

"The concern of public health officials is no longer for small towns like Donora. What happened there in 1948 is now happening in New York City, Los Angeles and Washington. If New York is struck in the same proportions as Donora, 12,000 will die, and 3.6 million will be driven to their beds."

Note that the specific number of fatalities and the number of bedridden convincingly illuminate the dimensions of the disaster. Then, Schalliol dramatizes the potential of similar disasters in denser population centers by quantifying what the equivalent numbers of dead and bedridden would be in New York City.

SPEECHES THAT PERSUADE AND INSPIRE

"Every time we try to influence someone's attitude in any way, we are engaged in persuasive communication," says Ben Brodinsky. But he draws a distinction between the speech that gets action and the speech that persuades. "It's a matter of intent," he says. "Speeches that persuade are concerned with changing attitudes toward policies and programs. They are what most business people call 'policy speeches.'"

These are the major speeches that business people give— to their peers at industry conferences and conventions, to graduates at commencement exercises, and to important civic groups and organizations like a Chamber of Commerce or a national association.

SEVEN QUALITIES TO PROJECT

There are seven desirable qualities of personality and character that should shine through such presentations, according to Brodinsky. They will help you persuade an audience to reinforce or alter its attitude on issues or problems.

1. *Sincerity*. To appear sincere, be sincere. Avoid subjects on which you don't have deep convictions. Base your opinions on careful study.

2. *Fairness and accuracy*. Acknowledge opposing arguments, perhaps even admitting that some of these arguments have a certain merit. One aspect of fairness is accuracy. If you are unsure of your data, say so. Vital point: Don't misquote or quote out of context.

3. *A likable image*. A person displaying warmth, friendliness, and good humor has a distinct advantage in all speaking situations. But in speeches intended to persuade, it's all-important to have your audience like you from the start. There are no simple formulas for successfully projecting these qualities, but your spirit of friendliness, with a touch of modesty, will go a long way toward producing a favorable image.

4. *A dynamic quality*. Successful speakers, especially those who give important speeches at large gatherings, are often described by words such as "energy," "enthusiasm," and "vitality." The listener sees the speaker as a person of action, someone who gets things done. Most listeners agree with the Greek philosopher Demosthenes, who said that the three foremost qualities in an orator were "action, action, action."

5. *Your expertise*. The surest way of proving your expertise is to be well prepared. Then, solid documentation of all your assertions convinces your audience that you are an authority on the subject. Don't forget to give the person who introduces you as a speaker all the data about your career and accomplishments.

6. *Respect for your audience.* Make listening to you pleasurable. Avoid rudeness or contempt for people, institutions, or ideas. Do not talk down to the audience. They may not be as well informed on the subject as you are, but there's a good chance they are just as intelligent.

7. *A professional attitude.* Professionals dress appropriately, conduct themselves with discretion, and avoid unnecessarily negative comments.

A step-by-step model for structuring a persuasive speech is shown in Exhibit 17.

ADDING POWER TO PERSUASION

Besides projecting those seven qualities, you can use the six strategies that Kenneth Wengrod, vice president of the Manufacturers Hanover Commercial Corporation, has studied in the corporate environment.

Wengrod divides persuasive techniques into six categories: benefits, consequences, praise, trade-offs, dialogue, and direct appeal.

1. Benefits. The first strategy on Wengrod's list involves persuading others by emphasizing positive features and benefits. This approach works to convince everyone else in your meeting—one, five, or one hundred—of the advantages of your plan, position, or advice. The benefits strategy works best on those individuals or groups who view themselves as "rational" or "logical" decision makers.

   Before implementing this strategy, prepare your facts and figures well. Document each of the benefits you cite with as much hard evidence as possible.

EXHIBIT 17.

A step-by-step model for structuring a persuasive speech

An effective way to organize a persuasive speech is to use "Monroe's Motivated Sequence," a model outline invented by Alan Monroe, a communications specialist. It is based on the belief that speakers can motivate their audiences when they clarify needs and then offer a solution that can be visualized and acted upon. Here is Monroe's outline:

Introduction

1. Attention step
2. Transition and orienting material
3. Definition of terms (if needed)

Body

1. Need step: demonstrate the existence of problem.
2. Satisfaction step: show how a certain solution advocated in the speech will solve the problem. Always be certain to use expert testimony, samples, statistical data, and so on to clearly support the points.
3. Visualization step: help the audience gain vivid insight into the desirable conditions brought about by the change advocated. In the visualization step, the speaker uses image-provoking language to project the members of the audience into the future, allowing them to visualize the proposed solution. For example, Dr. Martin Luther King's famous "I Have a Dream" speech concluded: "I have a dream that someday on the red hills of Georgia, sons of former slaves and former slave owners will be able to sit down together at the table of brotherhood."

Conclusion

1. Summary
2. Actualization step: ask the audience to take some action or to change their beliefs in the direction advocated.

2. Consequences. When the benefits strategy is inappropriate or ineffective, consider using the reverse technique. Emphasize the negative aspects of not following your suggestion or recommendation. The goal then is to convince the meeting participants that your plan or idea will help them or the department or the organization avoid problems or difficulties.

   If it's an outside audience, convince them that something negative will befall their "interest group" if your ideas don't prevail. The thorn in such a technique is undocumentable statements. You can appear manipulative rather than persuasive if you don't have the facts to back up your assertions.

3. Praise. This approach is a major departure from the first two and can be a powerful instrument that establishes a persuasive bond among individuals both during a meeting and afterward. The most important factor when using praise is sincerity. Without it, you get blatant manipulation, and the strategy will surely backfire.

   You must also exercise good judgment in timing (when and where to use this strategy), content (direct the praise toward relevant issues or behaviors), style of presentation (don't go overboard with lavish words), and follow-up (always try to follow through on both words and actions).

4. Trade-offs. The oldest and perhaps most effective form of persuasion is bartering. This involves trading things, information, or actions. But it only works when each party has something the other wants or can use. The more power you possess, the easier it will be to use this strategy.

   The danger surfaces when you make a promise you cannot keep or offer something that compromises your department or organization. Make sure all terms and conditions are clear to both sides. Don't be tripped up by some seemingly insignificant matter. This is the most common strategy in business situations. Use it wisely.

5. Dialogue. This will call upon all your new interpersonal communications skills. You must be able to listen, give feedback, offer empathy, and solve problems. Wengrod contends that this is more a style than a technique.

   The rationale is simple—self-interest. The more you seem interested in the opinions of others, the more receptive they'll be to yours. The dialogue strategy lowers resistance and builds trust. But it requires skill, effort, and an honest respect for differing opinions.

6. Direct Appeal. This strategy gets straight to the point. You state your position and ask for what you want. No beating around the bush. Start your meeting off with a flat declaration of desire. Wengrod found that this technique works with surprising frequency. Many people prefer to be asked directly for something; they dislike the feeling of being manipulated or set up.

   The major problem with this approach is rejection. If you get turned down or refused, it's difficult to revert to an alternative strategy. So use direct appeal only when you have a good relationship, when you don't have the time to implement other strategies, or when other approaches seem inappropriate.

One final note on persuasion. Don't let this important skill cross over the fine line into manipulation. Assess your motives and actions by asking these key questions:

• How would I feel if someone used this strategy on me?

- Am I being sincere in what I am saying and doing?

- Are my goals in the best interest of the entire organization?

- What do my colleagues think of my persuasive tactics?

INSPIRATIONAL SPEECHES

Inspiration is just as important to business as it is to poetry or religion. The best examples of inspirational speeches often occur at sales meetings in which the sales manager tries to encourage, motivate, and challenge the sales force to top performance.

The keynote address at conventions and conferences is another example of a speech that seeks to encourage enthusiasm. In all cases, the appeals are to common human qualities: pride and principle, economic and social goals, the competitive spirit and self-advancement.

Inspirational speeches are most effective when they are concrete and specific. Don't talk abstract principles. Set forth concrete objectives and rewards. Use vivid imagery that creates mental pictures. Slogans are effective, too. These prescriptions come from Brooks Fenno, the Massachusetts marketing consultant, who often speaks to salespeople to inspire them to heightened efforts. He cites a "classic" talk to inspire salespeople given by Arthur H. "Red" Motley in Richmond, Virginia. Motley has conducted numerous rallies for large sales groups and has been named "America's Outstanding Salesman" by the National Sales Executives Association.

Here are excerpts from his speech "Nothing Happens Until Somebody Sells Something":

The first thing I want to tell you men and women tonight is basic and fundamental. Unless you and I—those of us engaged in selling—retail and wholesale, printed and personal—understand what we do—and understand it in terms of benefits to others than ourselves—we will never do it well—we will always be vulnerable. The first thing that any man who is going to realize the great potential or capabilities he has in selling—the first thing he must do is understand what he is doing...

Understand what you are doing in terms of benefits for others and yourself and your immediate superiors. Believe in the product and the company you represent, and that takes some thought and some figuring—and accept the fact, like any good professional man accepts the fact, that you are never through. That's what I mean by being a professional.

And how do you find out whether you are a professional? I'll give you a simple test. How do you act when you are not selling? Let me illustrate what I mean. And watch for this. If you are a professional salesman, you are a salesman 24 hours a day for seven days a week. You don't just put it on when you get the body in front of the prospect and take it off when you leave his office. You don't put it on at nine and take it off at five. You are a salesman all the time. You eat, live, sleep, think and thrill to the prospect of being a want creator—which is the fundamental motivating force behind all human progress.

CEREMONIAL SPEECHES

The acceptance of a nomination, especially to political office, may well be the occasion for a major policy speech. But usually the "special occasion" speech—an anniversary, welcoming a new associate, saying good-bye to an old one—calls for easy amiability, not serious discourse.

In most special occasion speeches, you should strive to make human interest material—stories, anecdotes, personal experiences—predominate. Your taste in humor, drama, and good feeling about your associates and your business should guide you. The main point to remember is that there is a time and place for everything. Heated argument and acrimonious contention are out of place.

Here is how Orvin Larson, while at Brooklyn College, discussed the effective after-dinner speech. His suggestions apply to ceremonial speeches of many different kinds.

The after-dinner speech need not keep everyone laughing. It can be entertaining without being hilarious. It may be nostalgic; it may even elicit a tear or two. It may deal in mystery and suspense. It may indeed have a serious purpose. It may aim to inform or persuade, but if it pleases or entertains or thrills, it does its proper work.

Sometimes the after-dinner speech is left to chance, as if it were something unworthy of attention. Sometimes it is just a string of jokes without point. The best after-dinner speeches are carefully prepared; if someone is successful with an impromptu speech, it is very likely that at some time he gave that subject special thought or delivered a speech related to it. One of Winston's Churchill's critics claimed that he gave the best years of his life to thinking up his spontaneous remarks.

Suppose you are to speak to a gathering of public relations people. You decide to make light of the ways in which people try to get the best of each other in an argument. The topic is perfect for your particular audience. You decide further to give the speech a mock persuasive slant. You will urge your hearers to try out what you advise. You title your thesis "Five Ways to Win an Argument," and begin by saying that the advice you are about to give is guaranteed to work in all situations except disputes with spouses.

Next you outline your speech, formulating each point in the terms of daily usage, as follows:

1. "Let's throw the idea around a little more," that is, you try to win by protracting the argument.

2. "Well, there are two schools of thought," meaning your school is better than the other.

3. "We're really talking about the same thing," which prompts the reaction, "Yes, I guess we are."

4. "Let's see if I follow you; as I understand it, this is what you're saying." Your synopsis is your side of the argument. Only the sharpest opponent will see through this device.

5. "Try to see it my way," which means, there is no other way.

A good rule to follow concerning time is this: If there is no strong reason to talk more than five minutes, don't. Better to err on the side of brevity than to have your listeners look at their watches.

SPUR-OF-THE-MOMENT SPEECHES

You're at a banquet, and suddenly the master of ceremonies points to you. You're this year's recipient of the coveted "Manager of the Year" award! What do you say? Will you mumble "Well, thanks a lot" and sit down? Or will you deliver a polished, graceful speech of acceptance, thereby accruing added esteem from your associates and enhancing the reputation of your company too?

The sudden challenge of being called upon to speak brings rare opportunities. You're at a high-level administrative meeting and you are called upon to explain what to do about the decline in production at a particular plant. Or you are asked to describe how the new price policy is affecting distributor relations. Here's your chance to stand out! Few opportunities offer more personal promise or reward than a good impromptu speech at the right time in the right place.

PREPARING FOR
THE IMPROMPTU SPEECH

How do you acquire the ability to think on your feet, to give a coherent, meaningful speech on short notice? It's done by preparation, much the same kind of preparation that you put into scheduled speeches. For example:

1. Anticipate those occasions when you *might* be asked to speak. Analyze the audience, the occasion, the probable length of the meeting or event, the size, shape, and appearance of the room in which it will be held. Consider the purpose of the meeting. Arrive early. Find out what the room looks like from a speaker's point of view.

2. Rehearse potential material. Think of ideas, phrases, relevant comments, including jokes and quotations.

3. Listen carefully to the other speakers. Pay close attention to what's going on and what's being said. Think about how it relates to what you'll say if you are called upon.

4. Decide immediately on the focus of your remarks.

5. To the audience the point you spend the most time on will seem to be the most important. Don't announce three important things to keep in mind at the beginning of your speech, and then spend seven minutes on the first and two minutes on each of the others. Even though you planned to emphasize the three points equally, your message—as received—strongly emphasized the first. The audience will assume it was the most important.

6. Don't forget that body language—gestures, eye contact, facial expression—and tone of voice are essential

parts of the message you're communicating. A large audience may require more expansive gestures than would be necessary with a smaller group.

Eleven Patterns of Impromptu Organization

"Successful spur-of-the-moment speakers have the ability to organize their thoughts quickly," says Francis Allison, a speech coach and business consultant. "My studies show that they do this by applying one of eleven basic patterns of speech development to every occasion." Here are Allison's eleven patterns of speech development.

Pattern 1.   (Every impromptu speech could begin with steps 1 and 2.)

1.   Importance of topic to yourself

2.   Importance of topic to audience

3.   Summarize

Pattern 2.   (For a subject that may be discussed on a pro and con basis, such as a government regulation, taxes, education, etc.)

1.   Advantages

2.   Disadvantages

3.   Summarize

Pattern 3.   (For subjects such as houses, animals, war, government, jobs, cars, etc., plus the topics mentioned in Pattern 2.)

1. What's wrong with subject

2. How to correct what is wrong

3. Summarize

Pattern 4. (For subjects that can be restated as a problem, such as "What are the causes and effects of juvenile delinquency?")

1. Causes of the problem

2. Effects of the problem

3. Summarize

Pattern 5. (Same as Pattern 4 but in reverse order)

1. Effects of the problem

2. Causes of the problem

3. Summarize

Pattern 6. (Space or geographical arrangement—for subjects such as: customs, climate, governments, people, sports, buildings, objects, and even topics listed in preceding methods)

1. East to west

2. North to south

3. Top to bottom

4. Inside to outside

5. Any other spatial arrangement

6. Summarize

Pattern 7. (Chronological or time sequence arrangement, for subjects such as: storms, floods, civilization, attitudes, weddings, inventions, books, and topics listed in preceding methods)

1. First event that occurred

2. Second

3. Third

4. Fourth

5. And so on

6. Summarize

Pattern 8. (Historical approach for most subjects)

1. Past (give history)

2. Present (tell what is happening now)

3. Future (project your ideas into the future)

4. Summarize

Pattern 9. (Logical order for subjects involving a problem, such as, "What should be done about highway accidents?")

1. Importance of topic (tell why)

2. State a problem or problems

3. Discuss a solution or solutions (tell what each will do)

4. Summarize

Pattern 10. (Point-of-view order, for most topics or as an adjunct to the preceding patterns, for example, juvenile delinquency, crime, morals, movies, inflation, etc.)

1. Importance to self and audience

2. Point of view of a doctor, teacher, lawyer, minister, farmer, wife, child, banker, and so on.

3. Summarize

Pattern 11. (A more elaborate form of organization than many impromptu speakers would care to attempt, it is very well suited for a subject and occasion of special importance)

1. Importance to audience and self

2. History and development of topic

3. Current conditions pro and con on a local, state, national, or world level

4. Future developments

5. What audience can do regarding topic

6. Summary

Exhibit 18 lists the do's and don'ts of impromptu speaking.

Tips on Improving Your Performance

Here are some ideas for improving your performance as an impromptu speaker:

EXHIBIT 18.

Do's and don'ts of impromptu speaking

Do's

1. Take charge. Wait just a moment until you have everyone's attention. Then begin.
2. Choose your opening carefully, building upon the remarks of others, if possible, and then moving along to your theme and the one or two points that will support it.
3. Try to speak in a logical sequence, developing your theme chronologically (such as past, present, and future prospects), geographically (such as impact on Europe, Africa, and Asia), or by component parts (such as social, economic, and political aspects).
4. Search out any points of conflict or uncertainty and try to resolve them.
5. Define terms or make explanations when necessary. Relate new information to points already raised.
6. Choose your language carefully. This will give you time to think of what to say and will help you relax.
7. Relate ideas to the experience of the individuals in the group.
8. Be prepared to alter or adapt your remarks.
9. Be alert to nuances; pay attention to smiles and frowns.

—Approach the situation in the same spirit you would use in a conversation with a group of friends.
—Avoid tedious repetition.
—When you've said everything you have to say, sit down. Don't prolong the conclusion.

Don'ts

—Don't try to cover everything you know about a topic. Your remarks should be simple, brief, direct—not exhaustive.
—Don't be unnecessarily complex or controversial.

Don'ts

—Don't apologize for your lack of preparation and complain that you didn't expect to give a speech.

—Don't think you have to be witty or humorous to get and hold the audience's attention.

—Don't repeat yourself needlessly, wander aimlessly from point to point, or stay on one point too long.

—Don't assume everyone understands your jargon.

• Read the editorials in your local newspaper and respond to them. Say your thoughts out loud, limiting each reaction to about three minutes. Do the same for major news in national and business publications.

• Explain a process to a friend and then question him or her about how clear your remarks were.

• After talking with two or three people you know well, draw up a list of mannerisms they feel detract from your speaking. How can you eliminate them?

• Examine your own listening behavior. Do you allow your mind to wander while others speak? Develop an improvement program. Check back to Chapter 3 in Part I on listening techniques for managers.

HANDLING
INTERVIEWS AND NEWS
CONFERENCES

Depending on your current position in the company, its size and location, the "visibility" of your industry, and a number of other factors, you may or may not have yet had your first encounter with the media. But you've seen enough movies and read enough newspaper and magazine horror stories to know the grilling that can take place in the press. Someday you may be a "grillee." To avoid being tarred and feathered by an often unkind press, take heed of the following suggestions.

CONDUCTING A
NEWS CONFERENCE

A news conference may be held for a number of reasons: to announce a new company executive, the availability of a new product or service, or an expansion of facilities. It may be held in conjunction with a quarterly or annual meeting or a presentation before government leaders, bankers, or security analysts.

Whatever the reason for a news conference, reporters at a news conference will be seeking information about specific matters or events, and they will usually pose carefully worded questions. Your initial answers will help determine subsequent questions. Try to follow these guidelines when confronted with searching, even impertinent questions:

1. *Relax*. The reporters you face are just doing a job. Strive for a comfortable rapport with them.

2. *Personalize your remarks*. Instead of talking about what "the company believes" or what "we believe," speak as an individual. Use "I" and talk as an individual rather than as a mouthpiece.

3. *Keep your answers direct and brief*. Stick to the point. This will help you from stumbling into areas you know little about or are uncertain about. It will also keep you from rambling or repeating yourself.

4. *Welcome "naive" questions*. No matter how simple a question sounds, answer it anyway. Never laugh at a question! Your answer may be helpful to those who don't know your business well. Treat all questions and questioners with respect.

5. *Be specific*. Come to the conference with all the facts and figures. Be prepared to supply ideas and information in response to your listeners' need to write or produce a story.

6. *Avoid "off the record" statements*. Most reporters will honor such requests, but there's no guarantee. If you

don't want to see something in print or hear it on the air, don't say it.

7. *Remember deadlines.* Tell people at the beginning of the session approximately how much time they'll have. If you promise to get something for a reporter—a fact, a report, a memo—do it quickly.

8. *Use a meeting room.* It's best to use a meeting room or auditorium, rather than your office, as the site for a news conference. If radio and TV reporters will be present, be sure someone checks to see that the room can accommodate all equipment, including multiple microphones and tape recorders.

Distributing Materials

At a news conference, news releases, press kits, folders, brochures, annual reports, pictures, and other materials are always welcomed by reporters because they help with background detail for their stories. But don't distribute such materials ahead of time. That can result in a roomful of people who have lost interest in your remarks because their heads are buried in your handout material.

If the news conference has been called for the purpose of demonstrating a new product, you may wish to begin by showing a model in operation. If you do this, make sure that everyone can see what you're demonstrating. Close the conference by summarizing what you've shown and its impact.

Mastering the Interview

Interviews with the media pose much the same problems as spur-of-the-moment speeches. The main point to remember:

briefness counts. Stick to the point. Speak clearly and distinctly. Play it straight, using humor only when it's appropriate.

Tip: You can control a radio or TV interview to some extent by varying the length of your responses. Emphasize the points that you want to make, minimize those that the interviewer is intent on making if they differ from your own. Examples:

Interviewer: I understand that your next quarterly earnings report is going to show a sizable drop. Is that true?

You: Well, as you know, the report hasn't been released yet, so I can't comment on that. But I'd like to point out that our first and second quarters were the best in our history. Furthermore, the report you refer to would reflect earnings compared to the same quarter last year, which were also a record, as you know. Actually, we're still expanding nationwide. Our new facility in the west is scheduled to open next week, and...."

By such reasonable tactics, it's not too difficult to maintain a fair amount of control of the points you want to make. On radio and TV especially, always keep in mind that your time on the air will be very brief. Try to use that fact to your advantage.

Guidelines for Answering Questions

Here are some guidelines to help you give the best answers possible in any situation—a news conference, impromptu speech, or one-to-one interview.

What to do if:

- *You're asked a question that you can't answer.* Don't be defensive or reluctant to say "I don't know." Never try to fake an answer. Offer to find out.

- *You're asked a question that can't be answered in a reasonable length of time.* Condense or restrict your answer to only part of the question. If you must do this, try not to omit any essential details. Under no circumstances should you speak rapidly in order to make every conceivable point.

- *You're asked a question with many parts.* Regroup them into a smaller number. Use "signposts" in your response: "Still another reason is..." "A third important factor is..." "Now this is important..." "Not only must we consider X, but we should also be concerned with Y." Use summaries to reinforce what you've said and to bring your answer psychologically to an end for your listener.

- *You're asked a question you've already answered.* If there seems to be uncertainty about an answer you've given, try again. Then ask, "Does that answer your question?" If you still aren't getting through to the questioner, but everyone seems to understand and you can sense that the audience is getting restless, offer to meet with the person later or to have someone on your staff do so.

- *You're asked a question that you think is stupid.* Try to answer it without showing your impatience.

- *You're asked a question that is controversial.* Take your time. Treat key issues slowly and carefully, building your answers around them. Feel free to say "I must qualify my answer." When your answer is "yes, but" or "no, but," provide the qualifying statement before giving the yes or no. (Note: In preparing for any kind of a question-answer situation, anticipate controversial questions that might be put to you.)

- *You're asked a hostile question.* Stay calm. Don't try to discredit the questioner or resort to sarcasm. Stick to the issues and be forceful in delivering your remarks, without becoming overly intense. Correct any misconceptions. (Note: Sometimes it's best just to ignore the hostility.)

- *You're asked a question that you don't want to answer.* Carefully and politely say so, offering to meet with the person later if that is appropriate. If the person persists, try to sense if the question is one only he or she wants answered, or if most of the people in the audience would like a response. If everyone wants you to deal with the question, you should by all means try to do so unless there is a legal reason for you not to.

- *You're asked a question that can be answered with a yes or no.* Try to add a bit of explanation, or at least put the answer into a complete sentence to avoid giving the impression that the question was inconsequential or that your answer is impolitely brusque.

PUTTING YOUR BEST FOOT FORWARD ON TV

At this point in your business career, the closest you may come to television is in your living room. But times are changing. Video is assuming more and more prominence, especially in business-related matters. Just check out your cable TV guide.

Someday you may very well be on the other side of the set. So here are some pointers from an expert who teaches top executives how to deal with the most difficult of all interview situations—television.

Dean Thompson, film/TV manager of the American Express Company's Communications Services division, oversees two programs for executives.

The first is a one-day media-training program conducted entirely in the American Express television studio. The program is oriented to what business people might encounter when dealing with any interview situation—television, a press conference, or for print in a trade publication. The sessions rely heavily on television video-tapings of the participants and discussions.

Being on television can be a traumatic experience. When you're going to be on television, you're not always treated with the utmost dignity. It's not that reporters are out to make you look bad—it's that it's a very hectic and frenetic atmosphere.

I tell the executives, "They give you a cold cup of coffee, yesterday's newspaper, and stick you in a corner until it's your turn." Which is exactly what happens, and is what we try to emulate in our sessions.

In fact, I make sure that the crew does not do its final lighting and camera balancing until the students—the managers or executives—are in the studio. While I begin my opening remarks, the crew is running around balancing lights, pushing cameras, etc., and I say to the people, "Look, this isn't being rude. This is exactly what you're going to encounter when you go on television."

Knowing what to expect in a real television interviewing situation is the most important way to help the business people relax. "We teach them to expect the studio frenzy, and not to feel neglected by it."

While the program focuses on television interviewing situations, Thompson emphasizes that the techniques are valuable for all experiences with the press:

> There are traps that business people can fall into, traps the press can lay, and mistakes we all make. The television setting is a backdrop. If you see yourself on tape, it is not unlike sitting across the table from an interviewer from a newspaper or trade publication.
>
> But here you get the chance to see yourself and to be highly critical in a situation which is much harsher. And if you gain the confidence and proficiency to deal with a television interview, you'll be five times as good sitting across from a newspaper interviewer.

Media Workshops for Presentations

The American Express Communications Services Division also offers a general workshop to prepare business executives for any type of presentation. It consists of three sessions given over a two-week period. Rather than offering a set program, each session is devoted to whatever particular problems the business people themselves want to work on. Since classes are restricted to two or three people, instructors can tailor the sessions to specific interests and needs. This workshop also uses television settings and tapes as a tool for the participants, who keep their tapes so that later on they can work on mistakes and problem areas on their own.

Both courses offer a free two-hour refresher class within ninety days of completing the session. This is a "one-on-

one" meeting between the business people and the program staff, designed to discuss and prepare the person for a meeting or an interview that may be coming up.

Key to a Successful Interview

Thompson teaches the basics of good public relations and good communications. The most important guideline he offers: "Remember where you are and why you're there."

The interview is a 50/50 proposition, Thompson points out. And the interviewee does have rights. Business people may sometimes find it necessary to redirect an interview to get it back on track.

Example: The interviewer hasn't done his homework. He looks down at your biography, sees that you went to Harvard, and gets off on a tangent by asking you about your college days. But that's not what you are there to talk about. Says Thompson, "You have every right to redirect the interviewer back to the subject you're there to discuss.

"One of the biggest fears of business people is getting a question out of their area of knowledge or responsibility. And their biggest frailty is wanting to answer it anyway. It's perfectly all right to say you're not involved in that area or field and to get the interviewer back on the track."

Handling Tricky Questions

Says Thompson, "We try to teach the business people in our classes what they can, and cannot, expect in the way of questioning by interviewers. And we go out of our way to ask them questions they probably won't even be asked."

Some of the more common "tricky" situations Thompson prepares his classes for are:

- *The inconsistency trap*

   Interviewer to oil executive: "Four years ago you were trying to make us buy more gas, and now you're telling us to buy less."

   Oil executive: "No, we didn't say that." The interviewer then shows televised tapes of that executive, four years ago, saying "Buy more gas..."

   In a case of inconsistency in policy, Thompson explains, you should learn to say, "I was wrong." This executive should say, "Yes, we were trying to sell more gas four years ago, when we had it to sell. But we were put in a bad position by our suppliers, and now we're trying to emphasize conservation." Thompson's point: "You can be inconsistent. You can admit you were wrong. The public will respect that—it's more concerned with the here and now."

- *The absent-party question*

   "Did you know there's a Senate subcommittee that's been set up to investigate widgets?" (Executive knows nothing about it.)

   "No, I didn't."

   "Well, it's been formed and your company's been implicated for cornering the market. What do you have to say about that?" The interviewer may be fabricating the situation. The way to respond, says Thompson, is to say, "I'm not aware of any such subcommittee. If I were, I'd be happy to talk to you about it. As soon as I get intelligent information we can discuss it. But until that time I can't comment to you on what I don't know."

- *The "iffy" question*

   "If such-and-such happens, what will your company do?"

Thompson's answer: "When that happens we'll look at it and deal with it then. We can't deal with things that aren't here . . ."

It all depends on what the purpose of your interview is, says Thompson. "If you've been asked to comment on something, be well versed. Don't deny something that's true."

Tips on TV Appearances

Here are some tips to help you make the most of an appearance on television.

1. Make notes for review just prior to going on the air.

2. Learn about the studio environment before you go in.

3. Know precisely what you want to accomplish.

4. Watch the show itself beforehand. Try to pick up the flow, pace, and emphasis.

5. Practice any demonstrations you might use.

6. Practice giving short, quick, and lively answers.

7. Concentrate on what you are doing—not on how frightened you are.

8. Communicate with the studio personnel to make sure you understand what they want and they understand what you want.

9. Relax, but don't slump. Sit comfortably upright and stay alert.

10. Look at the host of the show. Give short answers.

11. Be animated. Use your natural gestures and expressions. Imagine you are carrying on a conversation with a close friend.

12. Be intimate. Talk as if you were talking to one person—the camera.

13. Notify your PR organization that you will be appearing on television.

14. Publicize the show in your publications, among clients, in trade associations.

15. Ask for a videotape of the show. Enjoy yourself.

APPENDIX A

A COMPILATION OF 101 WAYS TO IMPROVE YOUR PUBLIC SPEAKING

Increasing Self-Confidence

1. Be natural. Do not try to imitate someone else.

2. Seek out every opportunity to make a speech.

3. Never admit fear. Never apologize or suggest you are incapable of making a talk. If an audience did not want you to speak or felt no confidence in you, you would not have been invited.

4. Master yourself and your subject matter. Knowledge is power.

5. The person who wills to do, can do. Confidence is a state of mind. Be sure of yourself. Be mentally determined to be the best at whatever you do.

6. Believe in yourself. If you don't believe in yourself, no one else will.

Selecting Topic and Material

7. Never stand up to "say something." Always have something to say and then stand up.

8. Talk about matters from your own experience.

9. Always seek a definite response from your particular audience and select material that will obtain that response.

10. Make your purpose or response concrete, definite, timely, appropriate, and applicable. It must not be general, vague, or abstract.

11. Your material must be vital, concrete, varied, novel, and within the scope of the audience's experience. It must be logical and acceptable.

12. Quote authorities in support of your contention.

13. Read, listen, and study to obtain material. Observe, ponder, and have a healthy curiosity about things in order to get the best material for any speech.

14. Assemble 55 minutes of potential material for every 5 minutes of delivered speech material.

15. Always select your speech material with a view to finding an answer to the question "What can this audience do about it?"

16. Be original in your choice of material and topic. Avoid all platitudes.

Organizing Your Material

17. Reduce the basic reasons for giving your speech into main issues.

These may be:
Need
Practicality
Benefits
Is there a better plan?
Moral obligation.

18. Use the outline method of preparation. This will allow you to organize main issues with subordinate divisions of examples, illustrations, statistics, notations of authorities, and so on.

19. There are three sides to every possible question: your side, the opposing side, and somewhere in-between, usually the truth. Organize your speech material to seek the truth of the issue being discussed.

20. Remember that the informal method of speech organization is the most satisfactory from the standpoint of favorable audience reaction. The informal method means a speech well prepared but not written out or memorized.

21. Try to avoid notes. The exception is when using complicated facts and figures that must be absolutely correct.

22. If you do write a speech and attempt to memorize it, do not forget what you have memorized. (Remember, the written memorized speech and the written speech that is read are weak.)

23. Never take for granted that your audience is interested in you and your subject. Always create that interest through the organization of your speech material.

24. Never talk unless you feel adequately prepared.

25. Plan your first sentence with care. Use it to make the audience sit up and pay attention.

Improving Voice and Vocabulary

26. Open your mouth when you talk. Relax your jaws. Use your tongue and lips in the making of speech sounds. Create the idea that your voice manner is careful, easy, and spontaneous.

27. Speak from your diaphragm, not from your throat.

28. Never allow tight-lipped flatness of tone. Avoid stilted speech. Make your voice alive, pleasant, and agreeable. Your "speech personality" will depend to a large degree on the pleasantness of your voice.

29. Avoid lazy, careless articulation, enunciation, pronunciation.

30. Do not slur sounds or substitute one vowel sound for another.

31. Never let your voice indicate doubt, apology, or lack of confidence. Have an enthusiastic tone and sincere manner.

32. Avoid argumentative style and tone, even in an argument.

33. Avoid a mono-pitch or sameness of tone in delivery. Strive for melody of inflection in speech presentation.

34. Vary your speech rate—that is, speed up in some portions, slow down in others.

35. Avoid a nasal, high-pitched, or whining voice.

36. Use the pause between sentences. The pause affords

emphasis and opportunity for you to relax. Do not pause, however, between words and parts of words.

37. Avoid "anda," "er," "ah,'" "eh," "um" and similar interruptive noises in your speech presentation.

38. If your own voice does not appeal to you, why not change it? Listen to a voice you enjoy hearing. Mentally compare your tones with those of the other person. Try to change.

39. Increase your working vocabulary. Remember that the average business person has a working vocabulary of fewer than 4,000 words. Add 5 new words every day. Study your dictionary.

40. Use original, lively, and interesting vocabulary. Avoid slang.

41. Remembeer the ancient Greek saying that "a beautiful thought beautifully expressed is worth far more than any jewel." (Xanthes)

Platform Conduct

42. Be direct. Look at your group, not at the floor, ceiling, or walls.

43. Do not move aimlessly on the platform.

44. Never have unnecessary action. Control yourself physically. Avoid unnecessary head movement.

45. Keep your feet together.

46. Have a good position, one that allows you to be at ease and avoids all distracting mannerisms.

47. Avoid rocking back and forth on your heels.

48. Be careful of your dress and personal appearance. Be neat and well groomed.

49. Maintain your personal dignity at all times while speaking.

50. Show respect for your audience.

51. Avoid artificial gestures. A gesture must be spontaneous to be effective.

52. Do not play with rings or pencils or papers while you are speaking. Do not play with your hands while speaking.

53. Smile now and then, but not in a sly or secretive manner.

54. Give the impression of a healthy body and mind.

55. Never unleash your personal feelings. The average audience resents this.

56. Do not frown at your audience.

57. Recognize occurrences that take place in the audience or outside that might distract your audience or interrupt your speech.

58. Do not continuously drink water while making a speech.

59. Constantly seek the "yes response" from your audience.

60. Do not bore your listeners. If they read, look at watches, yawn, or fall asleep while you are speaking, it is time for you to go home.

61. Create the idea that you are having a good time making the speech.

62. Never thank an audience with a mechanical "thank you" at the end of your speech. Express thanks graciously. What you say is only half as important as how you say it.

63. Avoid all artificial salutations.

64. Always tie your speech in with what has gone before.

65. If you wear glasses, remove them while speaking. Most glasses reflect auditorium lights. But if removing your glasses would cause nervous headache, eyestrain, or difficulty in reading notes, wear them.

66. Use the Socratic method of argument—questions and answers—to increase audience participation in the speech you are making.

67. When you are through speaking, sit down.

Gaining and Holding Interest

68. Do not try to talk if someone is walking down the aisle. Wait until he or she has been seated before continuing.

69. Do not attempt to compete with people talking in the audience.

70. Recognize the heat and ventilation problems of an auditorium.

71. Walk to the platform in a manner in keeping with the spirit of the occasion.

72. Pause before you start to speak.

73. Stage props, judiciously used or referred to, can be attention-catching devices.

74. Never permit glaring lights, such as footlights or over-head borders, to be focused on you unless you are wearing theatrical makeup.

75. Use humor as a means of relaxing the audience. A funny story, in good taste, will help. It may arouse audience interest.

76. Refer to individuals in the audience, calling them by name.

77. For most speeches, get right to the point—usually within three sentences of the start.

78. When possible, mingle with the audience before you speak.

79. Make sincere and friendly overtures to your audience.

80. Do not be afraid to have good advertising beforehand about you and your speech.

81. Do not disclose your entire speech at the start. Develop one point at a time.

82. Use suspense to hold attention and have a strong climax to each element of suspense.

83. Use human-interest material—stories and illustrations of common people, common events.

84. Constantly vary your form of rhetorical discourse. (Use narration, exposition, description, argumentation.)

85. Have your descriptions full of "color" words.

86. Use concrete, rather than abstract, terms.

87. Use short words in place of long ones.

88. Reduce statistical information to a common element.

89. Use charts and diagrams to make your material clearer and aid in getting attention.

90. Use short sentences.

91. Pause after making an important point. When the point has "sunk in," clinch it, just as an actor clinches a scene.

92. Always talk so that you can be heard easily by all people in the audience.

93. Use figurative language—the simile, the metaphor, the analogy, personification, the parable, the allegory.

94. Use balanced and parallel sentence structure. Use interjections and exclamations.

95. Use dramatization to gain and hold attention.

96. Use the elements of oral expression intelligently, varying your pace, force, and quality.

97. Be natural. Never become wooden or stereotyped.

98. Convince your audience that you chose the subject of the speech after in-depth consideration.

99. The best speakers are always the best listeners.

100. Remember the definition of public speaking: The oral expression of an idea for the purpose of eliciting a desired response from a given analyzed audience.

101. *Be yourself*! It's easier—and far more satisfying—than trying to be someone else.

APPENDIX B

TESTING YOURSELF
ON A TAPE RECORDER

A tape recorder is an excellent tool for self-improvement in public speaking. To make the best use of it, Dorothy Uris, a speech specialist based in New York City, recommends that you:

- play back your tapes until you overcome the initial emotional reaction to your own voice

- enlist a friend or member of your family to listen with you

- use written material, such as this book, as a constant guide in your self-examination

To listen profitably to yourself, Uris says, you must also learn to listen to others—attentively and critically—by:

- sharpening your awareness of people's talking patterns
- tuning in to attractive TV and radio speakers for purposes of comparison
- making a tape recording of the best in TV and radio speaking for detailed study
- analyzing the elements that contribute to a pleasing delivery

TEST 1: GENERAL IMPRESSIONS

Make two 5-minute recordings, one by reading aloud material of your choice and one by carrying on an informal conversation with a friend.

Rate yourself positive (left column) or negative (right column) by checking the following:

Do you sound:

( ) Self-assured   ( ) Self-conscious

( ) Warm, friendly   ( ) Impersonal, indifferent

( ) Relaxed   ( ) Tense

( ) Fluent   ( ) Hesitant

( ) Genuine   ( ) Affected

( ) Clear   ( ) Slurred, meaning unclear

( ) Communicative   ( ) Unresponsive

( ) Appealing   ( ) Monotonous, colorless

TEST 2:
VOICE, PITCH, VOLUME, SPEED

Tape your reading of a variety of excerpts from each of the following, totaling 20 minutes of taping:

• a speech or editorial

• a short story or long anecdote

• light verse

Listen and pinpoint your particular faults:

Quality

___ breathy	___ unsupported	___ flat
___ graspy	___ tremulous	___ harsh
___ pushy	___ husky	___ pounding
___ thin	___ throaty	___ jerky
___ nasal	___ hoarse	___ not resonant
___ metallic		

Pitch

___ too high	___ too low	___ uncertain
___ monotonous	___ strident	

Volume

_____ too soft   _____ too loud   _____ muffled

_____ weak   _____ fading   _____ forced

Speed

_____ too rapid   _____ too slow   _____ dragging

_____ uneven, erratic

TEST 3:
ENUNCIATION

Tape the following test sentences as clearly as you can and with your best voice production. Then play back the tape, checking carefully to determine whether the italicized letter or letters in each test sentence are:

Positive	_Negative_
clear, distinct	distorted, indistinct
accurate	overprecise
produced with ease	pressured from the throat
placed forward behind the teeth	placed back in the throat
full, rich	abrupt, nasal
level, stable	wavering, drawled

Long Vowels

1. *ee*   Ph*ee*be s*ee*med to f*ee*l k*ee*nly St*e*phen's st*ee*ly gl*a*nce.

2. *ay*   You m*ay* st*ay* and pl*ay* another g*a*me, M*a*mie.

3. *a*   The m*a*n h*a*nded me a m*a*tch. D*a*d's l*a*st cl*a*ss was S*a*turday.

4. *aw*   Is Ge*o*rge the *au*thor of that st*o*ry? The *au*dience r*o*ared at the music h*a*ll.

5. *ah*   The c*o*p sh*o*t the r*o*bber while f*a*ther was p*a*rking the c*a*r.

6. *oh*   G*o* sl*o*w. The sn*o*wy road is fr*o*zen *o*ver.

7. *oo*   Is it tr*u*e that R*u*th had the fl*u*, t*oo*?

8. *yoo* The m*u*sic was be*au*tiful, as *u*sual.

9. *eye* The p*i*lot l*i*kes to fly at n*igh*t t*i*me.

Double sounds (dipthongs)

10. *ow* (*aht oo*)   Will you write d*ow*n the v*ow*el s*ou*nds n*ow*?

11. *oy* (*awt i*)   The ann*oy*ing n*oi*se sp*oi*led the b*oy*'s j*oy*.

Short Vowels

12. *e*   A fr*e*sh g*e*ntle wind s*e*nt th*e*m w*e*lcome relief.

13. *i*   *I*s T*i*m's *E*nglish s*i*ster st*i*ll s*i*ck?

14. *oo*   That g*oo*d-l*oo*king w*o*man baked the c*oo*kies and p*u*dding.

15. *uh*   as in accented position in words:
The tr*ou*ble was he m*u*mbled in p*u*blic and
no *o*ne *u*nderstood.

16. *uh*   as in unaccented position in words and phrases:
Alb*a*ny is th*e* capit*a*l *o*f th*e* state.
Laur*a* w*a*s *a*fraid th*e* defend*a*nt would be
*a*warded *a* thous*a*nd dollars.

17. *uhr* as in accented position plus *r*:
Did G*er*trude leave *ear*ly for h*er* j*our*ney?

TEST 4:
ARTICULATION

Check your pronunciation of the following consonants.

The Final T's And D's

Do you omit them? (Is your name "Packard" and you pro-
nounce it "Packar"; or "Kent" and you say "Ken"?) Then
practice these sentences on your tape recorder:

Di*d* you rea*d* the assigne*d* exercise, Davi*d*?

Haven'*t* you written to Margare*t* ye*t*?

Pu*t* the ca*t* ou*t*.

He packe*d* his bag a*t* the las*t* momen*t*.

The Singing Sounds

Do you slight these?

Ca*n* you na*m*e the tu*n*e the *m*an is play*ing*?

The gong sounded nine as William Lamb sang the last song.

NOTE: Be sure you linger on the resonance of m, n, ng.

That Liquid L

Is your tongue lazy?

Hello, Lola.

The newly built library is valued at millions.

NOTE: Does the tip of your tongue touch the bump behind your teeth every time?

The Friction Sounds

Do you unvoice them? Listen for the buzz

    z zh   z   zh   zh   z
As usual, Vivian enjoys the pleasure of leisure hours.
                  z   z   z
My mother drove five miles to bathe in the desert springs.

NOTE: For added vitality, feel the vibration against your teeth.

The Good S

Do you lisp even a little?

Sam looks so serious ever since yesterday.

NOTE: Is the tip of your tongue behind your teeth and never in contact on the s's? And do you keep them very short?

The Good R

Do you gargle yours? (or maybe say w *instead of* r?)

What pe*r*fect weathe*r*!

*R*obe*r*t and Ma*r*y we*r*e ma*rr*ied in the pou*r*ing *r*ain.

NOTE: Do you bring your lips forward a little and feel a slight vibration in the front of your mouth?

Smooth Blending

Do your well-enunciated vowels and clearly articulated consonants blend together into free-flowing syllables?

"We hol*d* the*s*e truth*s* to be se*l*f-eviden*t*—that a*ll* me*n* are create*d* equa*l*."

APPENDIX C

SELECTED
SHORT REMARKS FOR
SPEAKING ENGAGEMENTS

When I asked our chairman how long I should speak, he said: "Speak as long as you want to, but we adjourn at _____."

The secret of good public speaking is a strong beginning and a strong ending—and keep them as close together as possible.

An oilman told me the secret of successful public speaking: "If you don't strike oil in 20 minutes, stop boring."

Getting questions from the audience is like opening a new jar of olives: It's hard to get the first one, but after that they usually come pouring out.

A speaker took a very difficult question and answered it so artfully that he got a standing ovation from the audience. The same person asked a second question with the same result. Then he jumped up a third time and asked: "What was the third question you wanted me to ask?"—*I* don't have any such person in the audience, so go ahead...

Old age is that time of life when you know all the answers—and nobody asks you the questions.

Intelligence. The brain is a remarkable thing. It starts the moment you're born and doesn't stop until you stand up to speak.

Always tell people the truth. They probably aren't listening anyhow.

Don't be afraid to take a big step if it's necessary. You can't cross a chasm in two jumps.

It's not doing what you like, but liking what you do that's the secret of happiness.

Following the path of least resistance makes rivers and people crooked.

Exhilaration is the feeling you get after a great idea hits you—before you realize what's wrong with it.

Experience is what you get when you were expecting something else.

The most precious gift you can give someone else is a good example.

Leaders are people who know where they're going and can convince other people to come along.

It's all right to criticize people, as long as you leave them with the feeling they've been helped.

The time to start economizing is before you're running out of money.

You haven't convinced someone just by silencing them.

A good boss is someone who can step on your toes without messing up your shine.

There's nothing a good boss likes more than seeing an employee accomplish something the boss said couldn't be done.

APPENDIX D

FURTHER
RESEARCH OPTIONS

Every page of this book was designed with one purpose in mind: to improve your skills as a business communicator. To reinforce that goal, the following select list of publications and organizations has been compiled. It is far from an exhaustive study, but it should serve to whet your appetite, to give you an inkling of the further sources you can research to hone your skills to an even sharper edge.

Associations

Gavel Clubs
2200 N. Grand Ave.
Santa Ana, CA 92711

International Association of Business
    Communicators
870 Market St.
San Francisco, CA 94102

International Association of
    Convention & Visitors' Bureaus
702 Bloomington Rd.
Champaign, IL 61820

International Toastmistress Clubs
9068 E. Firestone Blvd. No. Two
Downey, CA 90241

Meeting Planners International
3719 Roosevelt Blvd.
Middletown, OH 45042

National Speakers Association
P.O. Box 6296
5201 N. 7th St.
Phoenix, AZ 85014

International Platform Association
2564 Berkshire Rd.
Cleveland Heights, OH 44106

Toastmasters International
P.O. Box 10400
2200 N. Grand Ave.
Santa Ana, CA 92711

Publications

Audio/Visual Communications
United Business Publications Inc.
475 Park Ave. S.
New York, NY 10016

Corporate Meetings & Incentives
Harcourt Brace Jovanovich
  Publications
111 Fifth Ave.
New York, NY 10011

Communicators Journal
P.O. Box 602 Downtown Station
Omaha, NE 68101

Journal of Organization
  Communication
International Association of Business
  Communicators
870 Market St.
Suite 928
San Francisco, CA 94102

Meetings and Conventions
Ziff-Davis Publishing Co.
One Park Ave.
New York, NY 10016

Successful Meetings
Bill Communications, Inc.
1422 Chestnut St.
Philadelphia, PA 19102

Meeting News
Gralla Publications
1515 Broadway
New York, NY 10036

The Toastmaster
Toastmasters International Inc.
Box 10400
Santa Ana, CA 92711

INDEX